P9-CEE-984

Coffee Break
Devotions

Fill YOUR Cup!

Blessings & Love,
Lynne & Tracey

Mother Child Camp 2009!

Coffee Break Devotions

Marjorie L. Kimbrough

DIMENSIONS
FOR LIVING
NASHVILLE

COFFEE BREAK DEVOTIONS

Copyright © 2003 by Dimensions for Living

All rights reserved.
No part of this work may be reproduced or transmitted in any form or
by any means, electronic or mechanical, including photocopying and
recording, or by any information storage or retrieval system, except as
may be expressly permitted by the 1976 Copyright Act or in writing
from the publisher. Requests for permission should be addressed to
Dimensions for Living, P.O. Box 801, 201 Eighth Avenue South,
Nashville, TN 37202-0801; permissions@abingdonpress.com.

This book is printed on acid-free, elemental-chlorine–free paper.

Library of Congress Cataloging-in-Publication Data

Kimbrough, Marjorie L., 1937-
  Coffee break devotions / Marjorie L.
  Kimbrough.
    p. cm.
  ISBN 0-687-08116-5 (alk. paper)
  1. Bible—Meditations. 2. Christian life—Meditations. I. Title.

BS491.5.K558 2003
242'5—dc21

                                        2002154382

All scripture quotations unless noted otherwise are taken from the
New Revised Standard Version of the Bible, copyright 1989, by the
Division of Christian Education of the National Council of the
Churches of Christ in the United States of America. Used by permission. All rights reserved.

Scripture quotations noted KJV are from the King James or Authorized
Version of the Bible.

03 04 05 06 07 08 09 10 11 12—10 9 8 7 6 5 4 3

MANUFACTURED IN THE UNITED STATES OF AMERICA

To

my new daughter, Adria, who I pray will be
strengthened by many devotional coffee breaks as
she pursues her legal career and solidifies her
marriage

INTRODUCTION

*A*re you in need of the inspiration that comes from meditating on the Word of God? If you are, then *Coffee Break Devotions* was written especially for you. Take the time to read each Scripture and meditation carefully as you enjoy your coffee break. Try not to rush. Give yourself a chance truly to absorb what you have read.

Because we so rarely touch some books of the Bible, I have chosen to write at least one meditation from each biblical book. I hope that you will become familiar with the often-neglected books and that all of your biblical studies will be enhanced.

There is power in studying the Word of God. Such study can change your life, encourage your heart, and strengthen you for your journey. Take a deep breath and begin your study. Breathe in the power!

BRING BENJAMIN

GENESIS 42–43

*Let one of you go and bring your brother, while
the rest of you remain in prison, in order that your
words may be tested, whether there is truth in
you; or else, as Pharaoh lives, surely you are spies.*
(Genesis 42:16)

*T*he brothers who had meant evil for Joseph by
selling him as a slave had to go to him for help to
save their starving families. But they did not know
they were going to see their brother. They went to
see a powerful man in Egypt who had saved the
country from starvation, and they begged him to
give them the supplies they needed.

Joseph had an opportunity to test their faith, for
he knew how much his father, Jacob, loved his
brother Benjamin. Benjamin had been left at home
in safety, and Joseph told his brothers to return to
their father and bring Benjamin back with them.

This was the only way they could prove that they were not spies.

Jacob was not anxious to give up his youngest son. Even though one son, Reuben, offered his two sons as ransom, and another son, Judah, agreed to accept full blame if Benjamin was not returned safely, Jacob resisted. After much pleading, he finally agreed to allow Benjamin to accompany his brothers. He sent gifts and double the money for the necessary supplies in hopes of having his sons returned safely.

How difficult it is to give up the one thing in our lives that we love most! What would it be for you? Is it a spouse or a child? Is it a pet or a house? Is it a car or some other material possession?

God has challenged us to give up all and follow him. He wants our total trust and commitment. What are we still holding on to? Sometimes we just have to bring Benjamin!

Lord, free me to give wholly to you. I do not need material possessions, and I pray that my family and friends have accepted salvation so that I do not have to be afraid of losing them. Remove whatever obstacle blocks my complete surrender. I offer this prayer in Jesus' name, Amen.

DOING TOO MUCH

EXODUS 18

*You will surely wear yourself out, both you and
these people with you. For the task is too heavy
for you; you cannot do it alone. (Exodus 18:18)*

$\mathcal{M}$oses had a wise father-in-law. This man
observed Moses as he listened to the complaints of
the people. He knew that the people came to Moses
because they wanted to know what God would have
them do. But Jethro, Moses' father-in-law, asked
why others were standing around doing nothing.

Jethro knew that Moses had taken on too much.
He needed to delegate some of the responsibility.
Jethro suggested a plan for teaching God's laws to
the people and selecting able persons to assist in
judging cases. They could decide the minor ones,
bringing only the major ones to Moses.

How often do we try to do it all? Is it that we just don't trust anyone else to do the right thing, or are we afraid that no one can do things as well as we can? It may even be that we are afraid that someone will do it better!

We must learn to delegate responsibility. Give your coworkers an opportunity to show what they can do. Let them know that you are counting on them, and compliment them when they are successful.

We do not have to be supermoms and superdads. Our children can help, and so can our spouses, neighbors, and coworkers. We wear ourselves out by trying to do it all. Take Jethro's advice. Divide the work. Moses did.

Lord, teach me to divide the work. I want to be a good servant, but I cannot be good if I am worn out. Give me the courage to share that which has been entrusted to me. Amen.

RESPECTING AGE

LEVITICUS 19

You shall rise before the aged, and defer to the old; and you shall fear your God: I am the LORD.
(Leviticus 19:32)

*T*hroughout the book of Leviticus, God gives Moses instructions for the people. They are told how to worship, sacrifice, live in harmony, punish sinners, protect their daughters, handle their animals, and eat clean foods.

They also are told to stay away from mediums, wizards, and fortunetellers who might mislead them, for God is in control. But in the midst of all these instructions, they are told to rise before the aged and defer to the old.

Our elders are to be respected, for God has granted them long life. And we can learn so much from them. Do we really treat our elders with respect? What happens when they are immobile and forgetful? Do we look for someplace to put them out of sight?

It appears to be all right to grow old as long as you stay of sound mind and strong body. But if you are feeble in mind and body, you are a nuisance to all around you.

Why don't you decide today to rise before your elders? Do something for an older person. Buy a gift; pay a visit; make a phone call; say "I love you"; ask about his or her life.

God did not mean for us to desert our elders. He wanted us to defer to them, to give them special favor. Are you up to the challenge?

Lord, make me more sensitive to the elders with whom I come in contact. Help me remember to show them special favor. Amen.

LIVING IN THE PAST

NUMBERS 11:1-15

We remember the fish we used to eat in Egypt for nothing, the cucumbers, the melons, the leeks, the onions, and the garlic. (Numbers 11:5)

The Israelites were in the middle of their exodus from Egypt. They had forgotten how they had been treated as slaves. They had forgotten how God miraculously had led their escape. All they remembered was how well they had eaten. They were sick and tired of the manna from heaven. They wanted some meat. They wanted the good old days. They were living in the past.

Sometimes we have selective memory. We remember the good things about the past and want to return to that time. We forget the bad things that happened and the new opportunities we have in the present and in the future.

Consider the past. Thank God for it, and prepare yourself to move on. You cannot return to yesterday. It is gone forever. Consider the present. What opportunities do you have today? How have you used your past to learn lessons that will help you today? Consider the future. What can you do today that will help prepare you for tomorrow?

The Israelites were so busy living in the past that they failed to thank God for the blessings they had. Maybe they did not have fish and fresh fruits and vegetables, but they had sweet manna from heaven. God had not forgotten them. They were blessed. Let us not make their mistakes.

Lord, thank you for today's blessings. Help me learn from the past and prepare for the future. I know that you were with me yesterday, are with me today, and will be with me tomorrow. Amen.

IGNORING THE REPORT

DEUTERONOMY 1

They brought back a report to us, and said, "It is a good land that the LORD our God is giving us."
(Deuteronomy 1:25b)

The Israelites asked Moses to send men ahead of them to scout out the land into which they should go. Moses agreed, and twelve men were selected. They brought back a good report, but the Israelites refused to enter the land. Not only did they ignore the advice of one man, but also they ignored the advice of twelve—one man from each of their tribes. Why had they asked them to go if they were going to ignore their report?

The Israelites believed that the God who had delivered them out of bondage in Egypt and who had fed them manna from heaven would allow them to be conquered by the inhabitants of the land. Moses told them not to be afraid, for God would go before them. Still they refused. Their refusal caused them to miss the blessing of the promised land, and none of their generation was allowed to enter. Their refusal and failure to trust and believe in God's protection caused Moses to be denied entrance also.

How often do we ask for advice or a report and then ignore it? God may send us a clear message that all will be well. All we have to do is step out on faith and trust him to provide for us. But we, like the Israelites, refuse and miss our blessing.

What report are you ignoring today? Is there medical advice that you are not following? Is there a loved one to whom you are not responding? Is there a job for which you asked but are refusing to accept? Trust God's promises; don't miss your blessings!

Lord, give us discernment so that we do not ignore the reports you send to us. Amen.

SAVED BY A SINNER

JOSHUA 2–6

The city and all that is in it shall be devoted to the LORD for destruction. Only Rahab the prostitute and all who are with her in her house shall live because she hid the messengers we sent.
(Joshua 6:17)

How many of us will miss salvation because we do not want to associate with sinners? Rahab was a sinner, a prostitute, but she hid the messengers whom Joshua had sent to view the land. Rahab knew that the land had been given to the Israelites. She recalled how God had dried up the Red Sea and allowed them to cross. She knew that God had made them victorious in battle because they were an obedient people, so she helped them in hopes that she and her family would be spared.

What if the messengers had refused to go to Rahab's house? They might have told Joshua that the only place they could stay as they viewed the land was the home of a prostitute, and they knew that he would not approve. They also might have refused to hide where Rahab suggested, believing that she could not be trusted.

What if the members of Rahab's household had fled for their lives, not trusting Rahab, a sinner, to save them? Perhaps they did not believe that she would think to ask for their lives as well as her own. But she did. Rahab knew something about the God of Israel, and she joined forces with his servants.

We all have sinned and fallen short of the glory of God, but some of us choose to make a distinction in sinners. We think that some sins are worse than other sins, and we forgive or excuse some sins but not others. We forget that one sinner may introduce another sinner to the way of salvation. Are we too proud to listen? Rahab's family was not, and they were saved.

Holy Father, there is none good but you alone. Teach us as sinners to be obedient to your call no matter where we hear it. Amen.

SATISFYING THE FLESH

JUDGES 14–15

But his father and mother said to him, "Is there not a woman among your kin, or among all our people, that you must go to take a wife from the uncircumcised Philistines?" But Samson said to his father, "Get her for me, because she pleases me." (Judges 14:3)

Samson had a special mission, which was told before his birth. His parents had dedicated him to God, and they did not see how allowing him to marry into a people who did not obey God's laws would enhance his calling. But Samson saw a beautiful woman and wanted her. He wanted to satisfy his flesh. She pleased him.

How often do we seek to satisfy the flesh? We give no reason for what we do besides wanting to because it pleases us. Do we suffer the consequences of our fleshly desires the way Samson did?

Let's think about it. Samson had been given great strength. His mother had not allowed a razor to touch his head, and he had had nothing strong to drink. He grew to manhood knowing that God had gifted him with strength and intelligence for a great purpose. He knew that he was not like other men. He knew that the Philistines oppressed his people and that he had a special ability to compose riddles. God would use all of these facts to bring deliverance. But why did he stray from his parents' wishes?

Why do we stray from our parent, God? We may have to answer, as did Samson, "because it pleases us." What we want and what pleases us may not be what God intends for us. Once we become one in right relationship with God, we can release our fleshly desires. What pleasures do you need to be released from?

Father God, we often yield to the flesh. Help us be ruled by your Spirit. Amen.

CHOOSING A NEW GOD

RUTH 1

*But Ruth said, "Do not press me to leave you or
to turn back from following you! Where you go, I
will go; where you lodge, I will lodge; your people
shall be my people, and your God my God."*
(Ruth 1:16)

$\mathcal{R}$uth and Orpah had been married to
Naomi's sons, but the sons and their father had
died. Naomi decided to return to the land she had
left when she married. She urged her daughters-in-
law to return to their mothers' homes and to the
gods of their land. Orpah took her advice, but Ruth
decided to choose a new God.

There must have been something about Naomi
and her life and witness that caused Ruth to want
to follow her and worship her God. Perhaps Naomi
had been faithful in prayer, and Ruth had noticed
her great strength in the face of adversity. Ruth

knew that Naomi had nothing, for she encouraged both of her daughters-in-law to find security in the homes of new husbands. She felt that she was too old to find herself a husband and have more sons. Her only option was to return to her home in Bethlehem. She hoped to find family that would provide for her. But she could not dissuade Ruth, and Ruth returned with her.

When they arrived in Bethlehem, Naomi asked to be called Mara, which means bitter, for she felt that God had taken all she had and had dealt bitterly with her. She told the people of Bethlehem that she had left them full but had returned empty.

But Naomi had not returned empty. She had been accompanied by her loving daughter-in-law who had agreed to work and care for the both of them. Ruth had agreed to worship with Naomi and her people. Somehow Naomi's God would provide. Ruth had chosen a new God, and he did provide!

Father God, help us be the kind of witnesses that will encourage those around us to choose you as their God. Amen.

Hearing a Good Report

1 Samuel 2:22-36

No, my sons; it is not a good report that I hear the
people of the Lord spreading abroad.
(1 Samuel 2:24)

$\mathcal{E}$li, the priest, was old, and his sons were evil.
He heard of the many evil things they were doing to
Israel and was distressed. He tried to let them know
that he knew of their evil deeds, but they would not
listen. They repeatedly sinned against God and even
slept with the prostitutes who served at the
entrance to the tent of meeting. Because they had
sinned against God, there was no one to intercede
for them. They were condemned to death.

God reminded Eli of the numerous blessings that
had been bestowed upon his family. God had delivered them from bondage in Egypt and had blessed

them in the new land, but they had been greedy in taking the choicest parts of the offerings the Israelites made. The indiscretions of Eli's sons sealed the fate of the family. God would raise up a new priestly family that would be faithful in keeping the law.

How it must have grieved Eli to hear such a bad report about his sons. What father or mother does not wish for a good report? But what do we, as parents, do to ensure a good report? Do we spend time instilling values? Do we discuss the temptations that surround us? Did Eli warn his sons about the prostitutes and greed that had consumed their family? Do we?

The only way we can receive a good report is to teach our children to uphold the law of God, but we cannot teach them to do what we do not do. They must be taught by example. The scripture implies that Eli had not been obeying the law of God either. He and his ancestors had been greedy and ungrateful, but his sons had been evil. How could he expect a good report? How can we?

Holy Father, we often fail to be the examples that our children need. Strengthen our faith so that we may boldly share it with others. Amen.

GET OVER IT!

1 SAMUEL 15–16

The LORD said to Samuel, "How long will you grieve over Saul? I have rejected him from being king over Israel. Fill your horn with oil and set out; I will send you to Jesse the Bethlehemite, for I have provided for myself a king among his sons." (1 Samuel 16:1)

Samuel had so much faith in Saul. He had anointed Saul king over Israel. Saul stood head and shoulders above the others, and Samuel believed that there was no one else like him. God had promised Saul victory in battle and had richly blessed all that he did.

But Saul turned away from God and no longer carried out God's commandments. Samuel grieved about this turn of events all night long and confronted Saul, telling him that he had been rejected as king. A new king who would be faithful and obedient had been chosen.

God told Samuel to get over it. Saul was not worth his grieving day and night. He had been disobedient and no longer deserved to be king. Saul was past history; God had already moved on. Samuel was directed to the house of Jesse where the new king would be found.

How often do we grieve all night over our mistakes and misfortunes? We need to get over it and move on. We cannot change the past, but we must prepare for the future. If the mistake was our fault, then we must learn from it and move on, praying never to repeat that mistake. If a misfortune befell us over which we had no control, then we must realize that God is still in control and will direct us as we plan for the future. We must not dwell in the past, for that does us no good. All we have is today; let's not waste it grieving. Get over it!

Holy Father, let us not waste the day grieving over the past. Strengthen us to face the future. Amen.

WHEN IS ENOUGH ENOUGH?

2 SAMUEL 11–12

I gave you your master's house, and your master's wives into your bosom, and gave you the house of Israel and of Judah; and if that had been too little, I would have added as much more. (2 Samuel 12:8)

*D*avid had been richly blessed. He had been anointed king over Israel. He had been given houses and land, wives and wealth. But he was not satisfied. He kept looking around for more, and he saw another man's wife and wanted her. He already had many wives, and still he wanted the only wife of another man. He did not have enough.

David did not stop at wanting the other man's wife. As king, he commanded her to come to him. She became pregnant by him, and he tried to make it appear as though the child was her husband's.

When that did not work, he had her husband killed. He did not have enough.

Nathan, the prophet, confronted him and asked him why he was not satisfied with what he had. He even suggested that God would have added so much more if he had only asked. But he had taken matters into his own hands and had caused the death of an innocent man. With all that he had, he did not have enough.

I wonder whether we, like David, are ever satisfied with what we have. Do we keep looking around to see what others have and still want more? Is there something in our nature that makes us want to "keep up with the Joneses"? Considering the consequences of David's actions, we ought to be forewarned that there is a time when enough should be enough!

Holy Father, we, like your servant David, often want what does not belong to us. Teach us, Lord, to be satisfied with what we have. You supply all our needs, and we really have enough. Amen.

HAVING GOOD INTENTIONS

1 KINGS 8

But the LORD said to my father David, "You did well to consider building a house for my name."
(1 Kings 8:18)

*D*avid wanted to build a glorious temple dedicated to God, but it was not to be. God let him know that although his intentions were good, his son Solomon would build the temple. It was well that David had it in his heart.

When Solomon dedicated the temple to God, he praised his father and recalled the promises that had been made to him. Solomon did not recall his father's sins, only his accomplishments. Solomon knew that as long as he and his descendants continued to walk in the ways of the Lord by following his commandments, there would always be a descendant of David on the throne of Israel.

Solomon also knew that the temple that was built for God could not contain God. He said, "Even heaven and the highest heaven cannot contain you, much less this house that I have built" (8:27b). Solomon was wise in realizing that a temple could be dedicated to God but would not be big enough to contain him. Although David had good intentions, I wonder whether he would have been that wise.

What are our intentions with regard to doing something substantial for God? Do we dedicate our lives, our time, and our work to him? What can we do today that will demonstrate our love for God? Even if we do not succeed in our efforts, will God tell us that it was well that we had it in our hearts?

Holy Father, it is our intention to please you. Help us succeed in our efforts and know that you are pleased with what we have in our hearts. Amen.

THERE WILL BE TESTING

1 KINGS 10

When the queen of Sheba heard of the fame of Solomon (fame due to the name of the LORD), she came to test him with hard questions.
(1 Kings 10:1)

$\mathcal{T}$he Queen of Sheba had heard about Solomon. She had heard that he was one of the wisest men in the entire world, that he had built a magnificent house for his God, and that his servants loved serving him and listening to his wisdom.

But the queen was not satisfied with what she heard. She wanted to see for herself. She wanted to ask Solomon some hard questions, and she wanted to test his wisdom and interview his servants. So she made the journey to Jerusalem. She came with gifts of spices, gold, and precious stones, and after gaining entrance to the king, she did not bite her tongue in asking him everything she wanted to know.

Solomon was equal to the task. He hid nothing in his answers, and his great wisdom was evident. The queen was more than satisfied and admitted that although she had not believed the reports, all that had been said about him was true. She further stated that not even half of what she had seen with her own eyes had been reported.

What a wonderful opportunity to rise to the challenge of hard questions! Solomon was wise; he was obedient to God; and when he faced the queen's testing, he was impressive. God gave him the answers at the time of the test. The result was that his great riches were magnificently increased.

Are we prepared to answer hard questions? If someone comes to check out a report about us, will that person be impressed with what is found? That person will be if we, like Solomon, follow the commandments of God and pray for wisdom and understanding. There will be testing; will we pass?

Lord, we pray for wisdom and understanding. We know that if you supply the wisdom, we don't have to worry about the times of testing in our lives. Amen.

WHAT ARE YOU DOING HERE?

1 KINGS 19

When Elijah heard it [the sound of sheer silence],
he wrapped his face in his mantle and went out
and stood at the entrance of the cave. Then there
came a voice to him that said, "What are you
doing here, Elijah?" (1 Kings 19:13)

King Ahab told his wife, Jezebel, that Elijah had killed the 450 prophets of Baal, and she promised Elijah that he would suffer the same fate as those prophets. Fearing for his life, Elijah ran away. He was so depressed that he asked to die, but God was not ready for Elijah to die. God sent an angel to give him food that would sustain him for the journey he was to take. When Elijah reached the cave at Horeb, God asked, "What are you doing here, Elijah?" Elijah offered a litany of responses; in fact, he held his own pity party. He had been zealous for God while the Israelites had forsaken their covenant, destroyed the altars, and killed the prophets. He was the only one left who still served God, and he feared for his life.

Before dealing with Elijah and his reservations about his future, God had to get his attention. Elijah was instructed to wait until God passed by. He expected God to be in the strong wind or the earthquake or the fire that he observed. But God was not there; he was in the sheer silence.

We may be running away from the problems we face in life. We feel that we have been zealous for God; yet, those around us are not listening to our concerns. We feel we need to get away. Perhaps a retreat or a vacation is in order. But remember Elijah. God did not speak to him until he was aware of and listening to the sheer silence.

Before running away, go into your closet, and listen for the voice of God. You will not find it in the wind that cuts through your soul or in the earthquake that shatters the peace you are trying to establish. It will come as you pray for direction. God still asks, "What are you doing here?"

Lord, I am listening. Speak to me. Amen.

36

HANDLING A DOUBLE SHARE

2 KINGS 2

When they had crossed, Elijah said to Elisha, "Tell me what I may do for you, before I am taken from you." Elisha said, "Please let me inherit a double share of your spirit." (2 Kings 2:9)

$\mathcal{I}$t was time for Elijah to end his earthly journey. The mantle had been passed to the new prophet, Elisha, who had listened to those who told him that the Lord would take Elijah away. But Elisha kept telling them to keep silent. He did not want to hear it. Every time Elijah tried to leave Elisha behind, Elisha would say, "As the Lord lives, and as you yourself live, I will not leave you." Elisha wanted to make sure that he was with Elijah when God took him.

When Elijah announced that God had sent him to

the Jordan, Elisha was with him. So when they tried to cross, Elijah rolled up his mantle and struck the water. The two of them crossed on dry ground. After crossing, Elijah asked Elisha what he could do for him before he was taken away. Elisha asked for a double share of Elijah's spirit.

What an awesome thing to ask for. Elisha wanted double the power that Elijah had. Knowing that all that Elijah did was possible because of his spiritual relationship with God, Elisha wanted a relationship that was twice that good. Elijah told him that it would be hard, but if he saw Elijah when he was taken away, it would be granted.

Elisha was determined. He already had stuck with Elijah from Bethel to Jericho to Jordan, and he was not about to leave him. He would be there when Elijah was taken away, and he would get his double share. He knew that he could handle it.

What is it that you have observed in a mentor or friend that you could use a double share of? You will have to stick close to God to receive it, but God is able to grant your request. Can you handle it?

Lord, grant us the double share of your spirit that brings inner peace. Amen.

IS THERE A PROPHET IN OUR LAND?

2 KINGS 5:1-19

But when Elisha the man of God heard that the king of Israel had torn his clothes, he sent a message to the king, "Why have you torn your clothes? Let him come to me, that he may learn there is a prophet in Israel." (2 Kings 5:8)

Naaman, the commander of the army of the king of Aram, suffered from leprosy. His wife's maid was an Israelite who had been captured during a raid. This maid knew that the prophet Elisha had the power to heal Naaman, so she told her mistress about him. As a result, Naaman went to his king and asked permission to travel to Israel to be cured. Permission was granted, and a letter and many gifts were sent in hopes that Naaman would be cured.

Both Naaman and his king had mistakenly thought that the king of Israel was the one who had the power to cure. But the maid had spoken of the prophet, not the king. When the king of Israel was confronted with a man with leprosy, he, in recognition of his grief and inadequacy, tore his clothes. Learning of these events, Elisha asked that Naaman be sent to him to learn that there indeed was a prophet in Israel.

Naaman went to see Elisha expecting him to perform some miracle or at least to ask that some difficult task be completed. Elisha did not even come to see Naaman; he simply sent word for him to wash in the Jordan seven times. At first, Naaman refused, believing that the Jordan had no miraculous powers and could not be any better than the rivers in his land. But his servant made him realize that it was foolish to ignore the prophet's instructions. Naaman washed and was cleansed.

Do we need to experience the miraculous or to accomplish difficult tasks to know that there is a prophet in our land? God has his men and women everywhere giving us simple instructions that will make us whole. Why won't we listen?

Lord, you have prophets all over our land. Teach us to listen to their instructions and follow their advice. By doing so, we too may become your prophets. Amen.

PRAY LIKE JABEZ

1 CHRONICLES 4:1-10

Jabez called on the God of Israel, saying, "Oh that you would bless me and enlarge my border, and that your hand might be with me, and that you would keep me from hurt and harm!" And God granted what he asked. (1 Chronicles 4:10)

*J*abez, like David and Jesus, was one of the descendants of Judah. Jabez's mother said that she named him Jabez because she "bore him in pain" (4:9). In spite of this painful beginning, Jabez was honored more than his brothers, and his bold prayer requests were granted.

What if we were to pray like Jabez and boldly ask God to bless us a lot? Somehow Jabez knew that God was not poor and had the power to bless him abundantly. We waste our time asking God for little blessings when God can and will pour out more blessings than we can handle. When we pray, let us ask God to bless us a lot.

Then Jabez asked God to enlarge his border. Jabez knew that he could handle more territory and do more for God than had originally been assigned. Can we handle more ministries for God than we have been given? Are we bold enough to pray like Jabez and ask for more?

But Jabez had not finished asking. He prayed that God's hand would be with him. Don't we want the hand of God with us, protecting and guiding us as we use his blessings and increase our ministries? Do we ask God to put his hand on us? Jabez did.

In the last part of Jabez's prayer, he asks God to keep him from hurt and harm. Notice that he does not pray that God will be with him and lead him through hurt and harm. He prays that God won't let hurt and harm even come his way. Jesus taught us the same thing when he taught, "Lead us not into temptation, but deliver us from evil" (Matthew 6:13 KJV). Jabez knew that God could and would keep him from hurt and harm. Are you ready to pray like Jabez? I am.

Lord, bless me a lot; increase my ministries; put your hand on me, and keep me from hurt and harm. Amen.

REMEMBER THE KINDNESS

2 CHRONICLES 22:10–24:22

King Joash did not remember the kindness that Jehoiada, Zechariah's father, had shown him, but killed his son. As he was dying, he said, "May the LORD see and avenge!" (2 Chronicles 24:22)

$\mathcal{J}$oash's grandmother, Queen Athaliah, set out to kill him and all of his brothers and sisters so that she alone would have claim to the throne when her son, King Ahaziah, was killed. Athaliah did succeed in killing all of her grandchildren except Joash. Jehoshabeath, Joash's aunt, managed to save him by hiding him in a palace bedroom and then taking him to her home until he was old enough to assume the throne.

As long as Joash was under the influence of Jehoshabeath and her husband the priest, Jehoiada, he was faithful to God. He assumed the throne at the age of seven and did what was right in the sight of the Lord as long as Jehoiada lived. After Jehoiada's death, Joash abandoned God.

Jehoiada's son, Zechariah, reminded Joash of the commandments of God and warned him that God had forsaken him because he had forsaken God. But Joash did not remember God or the kindness of Jehoiada, and he killed Zechariah.

We sometimes forget the kindness others have shown us. We forget because we are not faithful in keeping God's commandments. If we truly honored our elders and loved our neighbors, we would not be able to forget their kindnesses to us.

Remember today someone who has shown kindness to you, and do something nice for that person. Write a note, buy a gift, or give him or her a call. Show your appreciation. God has shown the most kindness of all, and we, like those of old, have killed his son.

Father God, we are often forgetful and unkind even when others are kind to us. Help us remember the kindnesses shown to us and express our appreciation. Amen.

RESTORATION THROUGH PRAYER

2 CHRONICLES 32:27–33:20

He prayed to him, and God received his entreaty, heard his plea, and restored him again to Jerusalem and to his kingdom. Then Manasseh knew that the LORD indeed was God.
(2 Chronicles 33:13)

Manasseh succeeded his father Hezekiah to the throne. Hezekiah had been a good king, but Manasseh tore down the altars his father had built to the God of Israel. In their place, altars were built to idol gods and were served. Manasseh was a very wicked king who reigned for fifty-five years and caused the people to perform many evil acts.

God spoke to Manasseh and to his people, but they would not listen. So God allowed Manasseh to be captured by the Assyrians and taken in bondage to Babylon. It was while he was in manacles and fetters that he humbled himself to God.

Why did it take a situation of great distress to get his attention? We are often like Manasseh, not remembering God until we are in trouble. It may take manacles and fetters for us, also, and we too may have to pray the prayer of our lives.

The Prayer of Manasseh is one of the hidden books called the Apocrypha. Although 2 Chronicles mentions the prayer, its text is not given. Referring to the Apocryphal text, the prayer begins with praise to the God who created all things and promised forgiveness and salvation to sinners. Manasseh confesses his unworthiness; yet, he implores God to forgive his sins that are greater than the sand of the sea and bows to God in total submission. He promises to praise God continually all the days of his life.

God heard his prayer and forgave and restored him to his kingdom. God hears and restores us when we pray in sincerity and total submission, confessing our sins and repenting. What a mighty God we serve!

Lord, we, like Manasseh, are unworthy yet humbly bow before you and ask for forgiveness from sins and for the joy of your salvation. Amen.

RESPONDING TO OPPOSITION

EZRA 4–6

This was their reply to us: "We are the servants of the God of heaven and earth, and we are rebuilding the house that was built many years ago, which a great king of Israel built and finished." (Ezra 5:11)

 ven though King Cyrus was stirred up and commissioned the rebuilding of the temple, there was opposition. There were some who wanted to help build but had not been stirred up by God. There were some who did not believe that King Cyrus had ordered the rebuilding. There were some who discouraged the people of Israel and caused them to fear building. And the rebuilding stopped.

But there were those who responded to the opposition. They could not let the spirit of God that had been stirred up within them die. So they resumed the building. When representatives of the new king, Darius, questioned them, they said who they were, what they were doing, and who had commissioned them. King Darius found the decree issued by King Cyrus, and Darius issued his own decree that the temple be rebuilt with all diligence.

How do we respond to opposition? Do we let the spirit that has been stirred up within us die? Do we have the boldness to state who we are and why we are responding to the spirit of God?

We need Christians who are not afraid to stand up to opposition. If God has stirred us up, he will see that we are victorious. He did it for the people of Israel, and he will do it for us. Respond boldly and courageously to opposition!

Father, you know how hard it is for us to face opposition, but we know that you are able to equip us to do so. We thank you for giving us courage. Amen.

FINDING STRENGTH IN GOD'S JOY

NEHEMIAH 8

Then he said to them, "Go your way, eat the fat and drink sweet wine and send portions of them to those for whom nothing is prepared, for this day is holy to our LORD; and do not be grieved, for the joy of the LORD is your strength."
(Nehemiah 8:10)

The people of Israel had returned from captivity and had rebuilt the temple and the wall surrounding Jerusalem, and Nehemiah, the governor, had inspected the work. He summoned Ezra, the priest and scribe, to bring the book of the Law of Moses and to read it to the people so that they would know how to please God. Ezra led the people in praise and worship of the great God who had so richly blessed them.

The people were so moved when they heard the words of the law that they wept, but Nehemiah told them that it was not a time for grieving. It was a time for rejoicing. He told them to eat, drink, share with others, and be merry, for the joy of the Lord was their strength.

Do we ever grieve when we hear the law of the Lord? If we listen to the reading of the law with hearts of understanding, we might grieve, realizing how little of that law we have kept. But if we listen to the reading of the law of the Lord with a made-up mind to follow that law, we might not be sad. We know that God is rejoicing because we have repented, and it is in his joy that we find strength.

Just think about a child who realizes that he or she is obeying his or her parents. That child knows that the parents are rejoicing, and the parents' joy strengthens that child. Even as the joy of the parent is the strength of the child, so the joy of the Lord is our strength. Find your strength today in giving God cause for joy.

Holy Father, I need strength, so help me live so that I bring you joy. Amen.

REFUSING TO BE
A POSSESSION

ESTHER 1

But Queen Vashti refused to come at the king's command conveyed by the eunuchs. At this the king was enraged, and his anger burned within him. (Esther 1:12)

King Ahasuerus had partied with his officials for seven days. They feasted and drank as he displayed his wealth and power. On the seventh day, when they all were drunk, he sent for Queen Vashti to prove that she was the most beautiful woman in the kingdom. He requested that she come wearing the royal crown. But Vashti refused to come.

Perhaps Vashti thought that the king wanted her to wear only her crown while she paraded naked before drunken and out-of-control men. If so, she had good reason to refuse. Perhaps Vashti knew what lavish feasts had been like in the past and did not want to be included in the festival. Or perhaps she was just tired of obeying the king's commands. She simply refused to be a possession displayed at any time and in any condition.

Queen Vashti had to pay for refusing. She was stripped of her title and was never again to come before the king. By refusing to think of herself as a possession, she had set a bad example for other women in the kingdom. They might follow her example and refuse to obey their husbands, and the king had to make sure that every man was master in his own house.

What would you have done in Vashti's place? Remember that she only lost her title and position with the king, but she could have lost her life. Do we allow ourselves to be treated as possessions? Do we respond to every request without regard for our self worth? Whether on your job or in your home, do you lose your self-respect by allowing yourself to be treated like a possession?

The only one we belong to is God, and he would not allow us to lose our self-worth. As Vashti knew, titles are not that important. Think about it.

Lord, empower me to respect myself as your child. Amen.

❧

WHERE IS YOUR WITNESS?

JOB 2:11-13, 16

*Even now, in fact, my witness is in heaven, and
he that vouches for me is on high. (Job 16:19)*

*J*ob had lost his family, his possessions, and
even his health. His friends came to console and
comfort him, but they had not imagined how great
his distress was. When they saw, they did not recognize him, and they just sat on the ground with
him in silence for seven days and nights. Then, after
Job expressed regret that he was ever born, each of
his friends spoke.

The first friend felt that Job had surely sinned.
There was no way mortals could be righteous before
God. The second friend urged Job to repent, for God

would not reject a blameless person. The third friend claimed that Job deserved the punishment, for he had to be guilty of great sin. No matter what his friends said, Job reaffirmed his innocence and called his friends miserable comforters.

Job finally confessed that his witness was in heaven and that God could vouch for him. He knew that his friends would never understand, but God understood. Job was a man of faith, and although he did not know why he was suffering, he knew that he had not sinned against God.

When bad things happen to us and we suffer, do we believe that we are being punished for our sins? Although we probably cannot testify like Job that we are blameless, we do not believe that our sins merit any suffering. Paul was clear when he said that "suffering produces endurance, and endurance produces character, and character produces hope" (Romans 5:3b-4). If we allow our suffering to strengthen us, then our witness will be both in heaven and on earth.

Lord, let me witness to others by the way I deal with difficult times. Amen.

A Fool's Response

PSALM 14

Fools say in their hearts, "There is no God." They are corrupt, they do abominable deeds; there is no one who does good. (Psalm 14:1)

$\mathcal{T}$he psalmist lets us know in no uncertain terms that only fools believe there is no God. Because of their beliefs, these fools are corrupt and commit abominable deeds. How easy it is to act as though there is no God, for if there is no God, then there is no punishment for sin. In other words, anything goes. Fools need not be concerned about fellow human beings because there is no God to whom they are accountable. There are no commandments to obey, and there is no standard for what is good.

The philosopher Voltaire said that if God did not exist, it would be necessary to invent one. We need God. We need rules and regulations for living. We need standards for right and wrong, good and bad. If we could not identify the corrupt and abominable, we would destroy not only ourselves but also our world. We truly would be fools.

But do we sometimes act like fools by ignoring God and his commandments? What about the times that we make conscious decisions to sin? Sometime we lie, using the excuse that we do not want to hurt anyone's feelings. Or we may cheat on our income tax returns. We may even steal supplies from our places of employment, and we often do so much more. Yet, we all believe there is a God; we are not fools.

We remain silent and inactive while people around us live in poverty. We are too busy to be advocates for abused children, and we close our eyes to the corruption in our courts. But we are not fools; we know there is a God.

I wonder what kind of world we would live in if every believer did the good that God commands. After all, we are not fools.

Lord, help me demonstrate my belief in deeds. Amen.

BLESSED ASSURANCE

PSALM 23

Surely goodness and mercy shall follow me all the days of my life, and I shall dwell in the house of the Lord my whole life long. (Psalm 23:6)

My husband's favorite hymn is "Blessed Assurance." This hymn speaks of the undeniable fact that Jesus is ours and a spectacular glory awaits us as long as we witness to the fact that Jesus is our Savior.

But who is the psalmist David was talking about when he refers to the Lord? He lived before Jesus; yet, he is talking about Jesus because Jesus and God, the Lord, are of the same substance, uncreated and coeternal. David knew that he had a dwelling place with the Lord, and his psalm witnesses that he had a blessed assurance.

During his ministry on earth, Jesus also testified to the blessed assurance of living with him eternally. He promised to prepare a place for us in his Father's house. And living with him in that house will be a source of glory divine.

What blessed assurance do you have? What are you assured of no matter what happens? I suppose this is a question that each person must answer for himself or herself. I can answer only for myself, and I have the blessed assurance that Jesus is mine. I know that goodness and mercy will follow me all the days of my life and that I will dwell in the house of the Lord, meaning both God and Jesus, my whole life long. What about you? If you cannot witness with David and me, then take the time to consider why. God's goodness abounds. Have you never experienced it? Everyday God shows his mercy. Have you been deprived of it? If you cannot witness to the blessed assurance that Jesus is yours and that you are surrounded by God's goodness and mercy, pray that someday you will. Remember that those who seek God find God. Call on him; you'll get an answer!

Thank you, God, for the blessed assurance that comes with knowing you. Amen.

HE'S MY LIGHT

PSALM 27

The Lord is my light and my salvation; whom shall I fear? The LORD is the stronghold of my life; of whom shall I be afraid? (Psalm 27:1)

What is light, and why do we so desperately need it? Whenever the power fails, people say, "We have no lights." They really mean that they have no power, but somehow, it is the absence of light that disturbs them the most. During power outages, I think about the light that God alone provides. When we are without God, we are living without light. When we live without light, we live in fear.

David realized this when he proclaimed the Lord to be his light and his salvation. Knowing that he lived in the light of God, he had no reason to fear.

He knew that he had the power of God's light to defeat his enemies. He knew that they could surround him and that he would be victorious. He could boldly announce, "The Lord's my light." David knew that this light would hide him during trouble and would set him high on a rock. As David's light, God provided shelter and protection.

The great gospel singer Mahalia Jackson sang a song entitled "He's My Light." Her light was that man of Calvary. She sang that she knew he had his arms about her. So she did not fear. Other words of the song are, "Power and might are his possessions," and because she knew that she belonged to him, they were her possessions, also. She had the same type of confidence that David had, and for both of them, power and light were connected. So when people say they have no lights, they really mean that they have no power.

Can you join David and Mahalia and proclaim that he's your light? It does not matter whether you are referring to God or Jesus or that man of Calvary; all that matters is that you are aware that you are powerless without him. Let the light shine so that you will not live and walk in darkness.

Holy Father, you are my light and my salvation. And because of you, I have no one to fear. Amen.

YOU CAN'T TAKE IT WITH YOU

PSALM 49

For when they die they will carry nothing away;
their wealth will not go down after them.
(Psalm 49:17)

My husband began his pastoral ministry in Chicago, and he was often called on by local funeral homes to conduct services for those who died without a church affiliation. Such was the case when a local drug dealer was killed. It appeared that this dealer had anticipated his death, for he had given precise instructions for his funeral. He wanted to have a very expensive casket, to be dressed in a full-length mink coat, to be adorned with jewels, and to have money in his pockets. He wanted to take it with him.

The psalmist was very much aware that we could not take any of this world's wealth with us; therefore, it would be silly to worry about the wealth of others. As wealthy as that drug dealer was, there was no Brink's truck following the hearse, and I doubt that his mink coat and money and jewels actually made it into the grave with him.

Why is it that we often are obsessed with wealth? The salaries paid to professional athletes could feed nations, and still they hold out for more. Those of us who make small salaries worry when someone else gets a raise. We respond as though that person's raise is being taken out of our pockets. Somehow we must learn to respond to wealth for what it truly is—just a moment's pleasure. We will not be able to take it with us.

Job had the right idea; he knew that he would not be able to take it with him; so he decided to praise God in his emptiness. Paul knew about this same concept when he announced that he was content in whatever state he found himself. I wish we could catch the vision!

Lord, help us see beyond earthly treasures. There are riches in glory that are not of this world. Amen.

CONTINUOUS PRAISE

PSALM 113

*From the rising of the sun to its setting the name
of the LORD is to be praised. (Psalm 113:3)*

I often teach comparative religion classes. I discuss Hinduism, Buddhism, Judaism, Islam, and Christianity. Whenever we discuss praising and praying to God, I like to look particularly at the practices of the three great monotheistic religions—Judaism, Islam, and Christianity. These three religions agree that there is one God in heaven and earth who is omnipotent, omniscient, and omnipresent.

Orthodox Jews pray three times a day: "Hear, O Israel: The LORD is our God, the LORD alone. You shall love the LORD your God with all your heart, and with all your soul, and with all your might" (Deuteronomy 6:4-5). And they keep the words of the Shema posted on their doorposts, reminding them of their devotion to God every time they enter and exit.

Muslims pray five times a day, beginning each prayer with "Praise be to God, Lord of the worlds, the compassionate, the merciful, King on the day of reckoning. Thee only do we worship, and to thee do we cry for help" (The Opening of the Koran). At least five times a day they are reminded of the one they worship.

Christians, however, have neither a specific number of times to pray nor a special way to open their prayers. When they experience distress, they may pray hundreds of times a day, and in better times, they may not pray at all.

I always encourage my students to develop a habit of daily prayer. I tell them to start the day with prayer and meditation and to send up balloons of prayer all day so that one will always be floating above them. I believe the psalmist had just such a habit in mind when he wrote that the Lord is to be praised from the rising of the sun until its setting. We ought to praise God continuously.

Lord, today I'll keep sending up balloons of praise. Amen.

WHAT'S IN A NAME?

PROVERBS 22

A good name is to be chosen rather than great riches, and favor is better than silver or gold.
(Proverbs 22:1)

$\mathcal{B}$eing from the old school, I have never understood the debate about whether or not a bride should take the name of her husband. I always assumed that that was automatic. But we are currently into hyphenated names. These names are so strange to us that we are not sure how to alphabetize them. We also have problems making them fit into the space provided on computerized documents.

Suppose the newly formed family decides to use the hyphenated last name. Both husband and wife will use the new name. Of course any children born of this union will use the hyphenated name. What happens when those children marry? Will they have double hyphens in their new name or perhaps even triple hyphens?

I know this is getting to be ridiculous, but what's in a name? The writer of Proverbs was not thinking about last names or hyphenated names. He was thinking of the reputation that accompanies a name. What kind of person bears a certain name? What good works are associated with that person?

Many expectant families carefully consider the meaning of the names they plan to give their children. I have heard people say, "Don't name him that! Everyone I know with that name is no good!" Again, they have missed the point. It is not the name but its bearer's reputation that is important.

A good name—one associated with good works—is to be desired more than riches. Alexander the Great knew that, and when a man accused of stealing was brought before him, he asked the man's name. When Alexander the Great discovered that the thief's name was also Alexander, he said, "You must either change your actions or change your name."

Lord, help us keep our names associated with the good deeds you expect of all your faithful servants. Amen.

MORE PRECIOUS THAN JEWELS

PROVERBS 31

A capable wife who can find? She is far more precious than jewels. (Proverbs 31:10)

When is a wife more precious than jewels? It is when she is capable, or virtuous, which is used in other translations. The writer of Proverbs is very clear about what he considers to be capable or virtuous. Let us explore some of the criteria mentioned.

This precious wife is always good to her husband, and he trusts her. She works with willing hands. She gets up early and prepares food for her household. She knows how to assign tasks to others, and she is a good shopper. She is not afraid of hard work, and she is generous to the poor and needy. She prepares for bad weather and makes sure that her family is properly clothed. She is so industrious that she even sells some of the clothing that she makes. She is wise, and her husband and children bless and praise her. She does not seek to be either charming or beautiful; she just fears the Lord.

This description is quite a lot to live up to, but I believe it would be beneficial to try. I wonder whether modern wives have lost the art of good home management skills. Are we good to our husbands, and do they trust us? Do we know how to cook and assign tasks to others? Are we lazy? Are we stingy? Do we prepare for a rainy day? Do our husbands and children praise us, or are we too busy trying to be charming and beautiful?

Each wife must answer these questions for herself. I still try to do some of those virtuous things, and I am encouraged by the praise I receive from my husband and children. Perhaps that is the key to finding the wife who is more precious than fine jewels. Praise her! Encourage her to give of her best. Let her know that you love and trust her. If she is capable, let her know it.

Lord, as a wife, I want to be a capable and virtuous woman. As a husband, I want to praise and encourage my wife. Grant our wishes. Amen.

MORE THAN ONE

ECCLESIASTES 4

Two are better than one, because they have a good reward for their toil. (Ecclesiastes 4:9)

When I was a young girl, I wished for an older brother. I felt that he could protect me from bullies and would be there if I needed a backup in a fight. Well, I did not have an older brother, but I did have an older sister. The only problem was that she was not a fighter. So, realizing that I needed a plan B, I recruited several friends to "have my back."

The writer of Ecclesiastes knew the value of having others with you in times of trouble. Think of being stranded in a snowstorm or being surrounded by animals or people intending to do you harm.

There would be no one to lie next to in order to keep warm or to help plan a strategy to defeat the enemies. The two of you together would have a much better chance of success, for one would always be there to lift up the other. And just think of how much greater that success would be if there were three of you. It's hard to break a threefold cord.

Considering the wisdom in this scripture, I know that I was wise to make friends as a child. I always had friends around me, and I never was afraid to face difficult situations. But I also learned that I had to be a friend. I had to be there for my friends when they were in trouble. Isn't it interesting how children quickly grasp this concept while so many adults try to face their troubles alone?

Take the time today to reach out to a friend. Make a conscious effort to be there for that friend. Someone needs you to be that strengthening force that will equip him or her to face his or her enemies. Someone needs you to be that third piece that will make the cord difficult to break. Will you accept the challenge?

Lord, make me the kind of friend that others can count on in times of trouble. Amen.

WITHOUT FLAW

SONG OF SOLOMON 4

You are altogether beautiful, my love; there is no flaw in you. (Song of Solomon 4:7)

$\mathcal{T}$his song of Solomon extols the beauty of the bride. Most of us agree that brides are beautiful. Even young women not normally thought of as beautiful are beautiful as they walk down the aisle on their wedding day. Just beholding them can bring tears to our eyes.

But as I think about this seventh verse, I must admit that most brides are flawed. There used to be a time when the white gown and veil were reserved for the first-time bride who was innocent, a virgin. Today, women who have been married several times and those who have been living with their intended dress in the white attire. Often innocence is not even considered.

I regret this new standard that embraces the loss of innocence and the presence of flaws. It would have been so nice to retain the innocence of childhood and to allow the young bride to come of age on her wedding day. We accept society's relaxed morality and agree to allow what had been a sacred ceremony to become tainted with secular standards.

What if we decided to encourage our children to live up to the description of the bride in the Song of Solomon? What if we let them know how wonderful it would be to be beautiful and unflawed? Their gift of innocence each to the other, bride to groom, would be the most precious wedding gift of all. I wish it were possible to reclaim the moral standards we have lost. Would you be willing to try?

Lord, help me encourage young men and women to be beautiful and unflawed as they approach marriage. Amen.

KEPT IN PEACE

ISAIAH 26

Those of steadfast mind you keep in peace—in peace because they trust in you. (Isaiah 26:3)

When one's mind is stayed on God, he or she is kept in perfect peace. This thought became a reality for me as I waited in the preoperative room a few summers ago. I was scheduled for breast cancer surgery, and because my mind was stayed on God, I was completely at peace. My husband had just prayed for and anointed me, and I knew that God would heal me. God's promises are true.

There was another patient awaiting the same surgery. She was tossing and turning and constantly calling the nurses for blankets and other items of comfort. While one of the nurses was trying to comfort her, she looked over at me and said, "I wish I could be at peace like that lady. She is so calm." The nurse responded, "Yes, she is at peace, and I want you to be that way."

The patient explained the many complications surrounding her case. She had been under stress because of her husband's cancer-ridden body. She expected him to die, and she expected to die, too. Because she did not believe that she would be healed, she could not experience peace. She did not have a steadfast mind that trusted in God.

I do not know how her surgery turned out, but I did pray that she would know the promises of Jesus and realize peace within her spirit. I don't know whether she was a Christian, but I do know that many who are never experience perfect peace. Is it because they really do not believe in God's promises, or is it because they allow doubt to rule?

Fix your mind on God: "Trust in the LORD forever, for in the LORD GOD you have an everlasting rock" (26:4). How comforting it is to know and believe this in your heart and mind.

Lord, thank you for minds that are kept in perfect peace because they are stayed on you. Amen.

❦

HEALED BY BRUISES

ISAIAH 53

But he was wounded for our transgressions, crushed for our iniquities; upon him was the punishment that made us whole, and by his bruises we are healed. (Isaiah 53:5)

*H*ave you ever had bruises all over your body? If you have, you'll remember how anxious you were for those bruises to heal. Everyday you check to see if the bruises have faded, and you wonder how long it will be before they are no longer noticeable. Have you ever considered whether the bruises heal us? Can we be healed by bruises?

I believe that bruises can be a reminder of our need to rest. We can become so busy with the affairs of the world that we fail to take care of our bodies. We become bruised in spirit. We ought to allow time for these bruises to heal us.

Isaiah writes of the one who is to come and be wounded for our transgressions and crushed for our iniquities. How many of us would permit ourselves to be wounded and crushed for the sins of others? We don't even want to be wounded and crushed for our own sins. We sin and want to escape without a scar. We want to get away unharmed. There was one who was completely innocent, but he bore all of our sins. He accepted the punishment that makes us whole. His bruises heal us.

Bruises heal us when we understand how the bruises were inflicted. Were we bruised when we rushed and fell? Were we bruised by someone who meant to inflict pain? Were we bruised as a result of an accident caused by driving too fast or while talking on a cell phone? How did we acquire the bruises? Once we understand and analyze the source of the bruises, we can allow them to heal us.

What bruises do you have? Will you allow them to be a source of healing for you?

Lord, Jesus was wounded, crushed, and bruised for my sins. Let me be healed by believing in him. Amen.

Are You God's Work?

ISAIAH 64

Yet, O LORD, you are our Father; we are the clay, and you are our potter; we are all the work of your hand. (Isaiah 64:8)

The people of Israel had deserted God. The beautiful temple where their ancestors praised and worshiped God had been destroyed, and all the pleasant places had been ruined. Isaiah asked if God would restrain himself or punish Israel severely. He pled that in spite of all of Israel's transgressions, they were still the clay that had been molded by God's hand. They were God's work.

When my younger son, Marty, was in kindergarten, he made a clay ashtray for me. He molded and shaped this lump of clay, painted and fired it, and presented it to me with pride. It was Marty's work, and although I appreciated it, I had no use for an ashtray. No one in our house smoked, and there were no ashtrays around. The ashtray was not useful, but it was loved because it was Marty's work.

Are we useful to God, or do we want to be loved just because we are God's work? Isaiah knew that Israel was not useful to God. The Israelites no longer worshiped or served God, but Isaiah reminded God that they were God's work. God was the potter, and the Israelites were the clay. Even though the Israelites were not useful to God, Isaiah wanted God to keep blessing them.

We are like Isaiah in our prayers and pleas to God. Regardless of our usefulness to God, we still want God to bless us. We may never praise or worship God, but we expect God to be there for us because we are his work. God expects praise, adoration, and service, but we do not treat God fairly. Let us resolve to give praise, adoration, and service to him, for as we praise and serve, we truly become God's work.

Lord, help me be not only faithful but also useful to you. Amen.

☙☙

LOOKING FORWARD

JEREMIAH 7

Yet they did not obey or incline their ear, but, in the stubbornness of their evil will, they walked in their own counsels, and looked backward rather than forward. (Jeremiah 7:24)

Jeremiah makes a strong indictment in this sentence. The people of Israel are guilty of many wrongs, and most of them are given here. Let's consider those wrongs and see how many we share.

First, they were disobedient and did not listen. How often are we guilty of the same thing? We fail to obey the instructions given by our doctors, and we eat things that are harmful to our bodies. We fail to obey the speed limit, endangering our lives as well as the lives of others. We do not take the time to listen to our elders or to our children. We are too busy to listen to others and believe that we really don't need to listen to them anyway because we have all the answers.

Second, the Israelites were so stubborn and evil that they just followed their own advice. Isn't it interesting that when we fail to listen to others, we have only our own counsel to guide us? If we are evil, as were the Israelites, the counsel we are following is not beneficial. God had given the Israelites all the counsel they would ever need, but they were too stubborn to follow it. I hope we are not that stubborn.

Third, the Israelites looked backward rather than forward. How often are we reminded that looking backward leads to death and destruction? We all remember Lot's wife. She was disobedient and stubborn; she looked back and died because of that. We often want to look back. We remember what we call the "good old days," but I wonder how good those days really were. There is no benefit in looking back. No matter how good those days were, we will never experience them again. We need to look forward. We will have opportunities to follow God's counsel in the future. Look forward!

Lord, teach me to be obedient, to listen, to turn away from evil, and to look forward to a future serving you. Amen.

இ

A Word from the Lord

Jeremiah 20, 37, and 52

Then King Zedekiah sent for him, and received him. The king questioned him secretly in his house, and said, "Is there any word from the Lord?" Jeremiah said, "There is!" Then he said, "You shall be handed over to the king of Babylon." (Jeremiah 37:17)

Jeremiah felt compelled to preach the word of God. Even though the people mocked him, he still preached. He said, "If I say, 'I will not mention him, or speak any more in his name,' then within me there is something like a burning fire shut up in my bones; I am weary with holding it in, and I cannot" (20:9). What a marvelous thing to be so called by God that the message just burns to get out. So Jeremiah let that message out and was imprisoned on the charge that he was deserting to the Chaldeans.

After Jeremiah had been beaten and held captive for many days, King Zedekiah sent for him. I find it quite interesting that after no one wanted to hear what Jeremiah had to say, this king asked if there was a word from the Lord. Because Jeremiah could not keep that word shut up in his bones, he responded, "There is!" and told the king that he would be handed over to the king of Babylon. I am sure that his being captured was not the word that King Zedekiah wanted to hear. But Jeremiah, though his fate was in the hands of King Zedekiah, delivered the word that God had given him. Zedekiah was indeed captured, his sons were killed in front of him, his eyes were put out, and he remained in prison until his death.

How many of us accurately receive the word of God that is boldly preached. We often ask, "Is there a word from the Lord?" but may not listen to it. When a true servant of the Lord preaches and delivers God's word, a word that just burns to get out, we need to listen and respond accordingly. If there is a word from the Lord, internalize it!

Lord, help me recognize and respond to your word when one who just cannot hold it in preaches it. Amen.

LIMITED REJECTION

LAMENTATIONS 3

Although he causes grief, he will have compassion
according to the abundance of his steadfast love.
(Lamentations 3:32)

*I*n this same chapter of the book of
Lamentations, Jeremiah remembers the sins of
Israel and grieves for her past days of glory. He
recalls how deserted Jerusalem is and how great her
transgressions are. He feels that his calls for help
and his prayers to God have been shut out. Yet, he
knows that God's love never ceases and that he and
all of Israel must wait quietly for salvation.

Jeremiah boldly states, "For the Lord will not
reject forever" (3:31). He knows that God eventually will have compassion because "he does not

willingly afflict or grieve anyone" (3:33). God's rejection is limited; he just waits for us to get our act together.

Jeremiah's lament could be for any of us, for all have sinned and fallen short of God's glory. I know that we feel rejected at times and believe that God does not hear our prayers. Perhaps we are not praying with a spirit of willingness to repent and respond to God's direction. No matter what state we find ourselves in, we are reminded that because of God's abundant love, he will have compassion.

I wonder how many of us have enough love and compassion to forgive those who have wronged us. I know that unlike God, most of us reject others. Once someone has caused us pain, we never again seek to love and forgive him or her. Whatever that person did to us could not compare with Israel's sins against God. What we need is just a fraction of God's love and compassion. Resolve today to forgive someone against whom you have ill will. Let your rejection of him or her be limited.

Lord, give me a forgiving spirit. Amen.

PERSONAL SIN
AND RIGHTEOUSNESS

EZEKIEL 18

*The person who sins shall die. A child shall not
suffer for the iniquity of a parent, nor a parent
suffer for the iniquity of a child; the righteousness
of the righteous shall be his own, and the
wickedness of the wicked shall be his own.
(Ezekiel 18:20)*

In a recent criminal case, a convicted criminal
paid a man to serve his prison sentence for him. The
innocent man assumed the identity of the criminal
and went to jail. They got away with it for a few
years, but they eventually were caught. The man
who served the time for the criminal was paid
$50,000, but once they were discovered, both men
were charged with fraud. They learned the hard way
that each person has to serve his own time for the
sins that he or she has committed.

Although we may understand the criminal wanting someone to serve his prison time, I wonder whether he would have paid $50,000 to someone to assume his place if he were being honored for his righteousness or glory.

Ezekiel prophesied to Israel concerning personal sin and righteousness. He listed in detail the many sins that were and still are in direct disobedience to the ordinances of God. He let them know that children do not suffer for the sins of their parents and that parents do not suffer for their children. In like manner, he made sure that they knew that it is not possible to claim the righteousness of others. We suffer for our own sins and enjoy the fruits of our own righteousness.

Have you ever wanted to trade places with someone? Would you consider assuming their wickedness and their righteousness? I would not; I will take my chances with my own sins, for Ezekiel has told me that God will not remember my transgressions if I turn away from them and obey God. Years later, Jesus confirmed this prophecy by offering his body in atonement for my sins.

Father, I thank you for forgetting my sins and remembering my righteousness. Keep me aware of my personal responsibility to you for all that you do. Amen.

THE WRITING ON THE WALL

DANIEL 4:28–5

*Then Daniel answered in the presence of the king,
"Let your gifts be for yourself, or give your
rewards to someone else! Nevertheless I will read
the writing to the king and let him know the
interpretation." (Daniel 5:17)*

Belshazzar succeeded his father, Nebuchadnezzar, as king. For a time, Nebuchadnezzar had
been removed from his throne because he began to
believe that he alone was responsible for his position
and power. God had humbled Nebuchadnezzar by
removing him from human society and causing him
to live and eat with animals and to bathe with the
dew of heaven. He had to live that way until he realized
that God was sovereign and worthy of praise.

It seemed that Belshazzar had not learned from
his father's mistakes, and he and his assembled

company praised the gods of silver, bronze, iron, wood, and stone. God responded to Belshazzar's actions by sending a human hand to write on the wall of the royal palace. No one could interpret the writing even though the king offered fine gifts as a reward. It was the queen who told the king about the wisdom of Daniel, and Daniel was summoned.

The king tried to offer gifts to Daniel in payment for the interpretation of the writing, but Daniel did not need a reward. Daniel let him know that the days of his kingdom were numbered, that he had been weighed and found wanting, and that his kingdom would be divided and given to others. This interpretation proved true, and Belshazzar was killed that very night.

Daniel was brave enough to announce the shortcomings of the king. He was bold in his proclamation, and the king's greatest fears were realized. When we see others worshiping false images of silver and gold and so many other things, do we witness to the sovereignty of God and the uselessness of idols? Daniel challenges us to read the writing on the wall to those who fail to worship God.

Lord, keep me humble and knowledgeable of your sovereignty, and give me courage to witness to those who are not serving you. Amen.

GOD'S INDICTMENT

HOSEA 4:1-3

*Hear the word of the LORD, O people of Israel; for
the LORD has an indictment against the
inhabitants of the land. There is no faithfulness or
loyalty, and no knowledge of God in the land.
(Hosea 4:1)*

Hosea spoke out for God. He let the people
of Israel know that God was very disappointed in
them. In fact, there was an indictment against
them. The indictment included unfaithfulness, dis-
loyalty, and ignorance of God.

How like the people of Israel we are. Would not
an indictment of the people of America contain the
same complaints? Surely the indictment against
America would include being unfaithful, disloyal,
and ignorant of God. What can we do to change
these circumstances?

Well, Hosea told the people of Israel that they had to give up their idols and return to God. We, in America, are so like those Israelites. We have failed to worship God while we spend our time with our idols of houses and cars and money and drugs. We spend our time studying sports and acting as Monday-morning quarterbacks; we memorize the television schedules and fail to memorize Scripture; we take pride in having manicured laws and preparing gourmet meals, but we do not invest in getting to know, love, and serve the God who has given all of these things to us.

Hosea gave a call to repentance, "Come, let us return to the LORD; for it is he who has torn, and he will heal us; he has struck down, and . . . he will raise us up, that we may live before him" (6:1-2). He made it clear that only God could restore the Israelites and only God can restore the Americans.

Lord, we, like those who have gone before us, sometimes bow down to other gods. Give us the spirit of obedience to you and you alone. Amen.

PAYBACK TIME

JOEL 3:1-8

What are you to me, O Tyre and Sidon, and all the regions of Philistia? Are you paying me back for something? If you are paying me back, I will turn your deeds back upon your own heads swiftly and speedily. (Joel 3:4)

ave you ever wondered what would happen to you if God decided that it was payback time? What if our deeds were turned back upon our own heads and we had to take whatever punishment accompanied them? What if we had to suffer the consequences every time we disobeyed a rule or a law?

Just think about it. How many times have you disregarded the speed limits or missed having an accident just by inches? You could have been killed or you could have killed or maimed someone else, but that awesome God we serve did not turn those deeds back on us. Even though we were spared, how many of us bothered to give God the praise, thanksgiving, and worship that was so deserved. Wouldn't that have been worthy payback from us to God?

How often do we vow to seek revenge on someone who has told a lie on us or cheated us out of money or position? Are we thinking that it's payback time? I wonder whether we consider the many times we have cheated God out of our tithe or the primary place of devotion in our lives. I remember wanting a payback from a man who sold me a car he did not own. Although he cashed my check, the police came for the car. I was left with nothing. I took the matter to the authorities, and the judge ruled that I was due retribution. However, the man made only a few payments before he was jailed for another crime. I thought about it and decided that the money I lost was already God's and additional monies I received were already God's too. I did not need to think about payback because I would never be able to pay God back. None of us could.

Lord, keep me from being guilty of seeking payback from others. We owe you far too much to be concerned about anything but your continuous praise and worship. Amen.

Do We Need a Plumb Line?

Amos 7:7-9

And the L<small>ORD</small> said to me, "Amos, what do you see?" And I said, "A plumb line." Then the Lord said, "See, I am setting a plumb line in the midst of my people Israel; I will never again pass them by." (Amos 7:8)

A plumb line is a line of cord with a weight at one end that is used either to determine if something is vertical or to measure its depth. It may also be used to determine whether a wall is being built straight and true. The plumb line can be used to measure the wall and discover where it is crooked. The crooked places may have to be torn down and rebuilt.

Amos saw a plumb line, which God had set in the midst of his people. The people would be measured by the plumb line's standard. The crooked and corrupt people would be judged and punished. God would no longer pass them by or forgive their wickedness. God's patience had come to an end. It was time to be measured by the correct standard.

Do we need a plumb line? Do we need a measure to show the places where we bulge and depart from God's rule? I am sure that we already know of several ways in which we fail to be straight and true, but who is measuring us by God's plumb line? We might think that the clergy use God's plumb line and hold us to its standard, but what about the standards to which they hold themselves? With allegations of sexual abuse inflicted by various members of the clergy and the theft of church funds, can we really trust the clergy to see and use God's plumb line?

I am sure that we do not want God to set his plumb line in our midst, for all of us would fail to meet its standard. Perhaps we should start to use God's plumb line and daily measure ourselves against God's standard.

Lord, I want to be a wall standing straight and erect for you. Make me a plumb line. Amen.

FALLING FROM HIGH PLACES

OBADIAH 1-4

Your proud heart has deceived you, you that live in the clefts of the rock, whose dwelling is in the heights. You say in your heart, "Who will bring me down to the ground?" (Obadiah 3)

Obadiah is the shortest book in the Old Testament, and it contains the vision of the prophet Obadiah. This vision is directed toward the Edomites, but it contains wisdom for all. Essentially we learn that no matter how high we believe we have risen, we can be brought down.

This message is especially true today, when we see large corporations fall due to the mismanagement of funds and insider stock trading. Executives who once lived in multimillion-dollar mansions are forced to move to small apartments. Thousands of employees lose their jobs, and many lose their life savings. Yes, it is easy to fall from high places.

Perhaps Obadiah is speaking to our generation. He is telling us that "the kingdom shall be the LORD's" (v. 21*b*); and unless we dwell with the Lord and live in his kingdom, we will lose all that we have.

This is a hard pill to swallow because, like the rich young ruler (in Matthew 19:16-26), some of us have great possessions. But what good are all the things that we have when we may lose our very souls? Obadiah warns us that no matter how high we soar, even as high as an eagle, we can be brought down. Just think, if we take God with us on our way up, he will be with us on our way down. The fall won't hurt nearly as bad if God is with us. We ought to live in such a way that we are never out of his loving care.

Lord, if it is your will that I soar to high places, be with me if I fall down. I know that with your help I can get back up. Amen.

ONE LIFE FOR MANY

JONAH 1:11-17

*He said to them, "Pick me up and throw me into
the sea; then the sea will quiet down for you; for I
know it is because of me that this great storm has
come upon you." (Jonah 1:12)*

$\mathcal{J}$ust imagine the mariners' distress when
they discovered that Jonah was the cause of the
great storm that had them frightened for their lives.
Jonah was well aware that he was to blame, and the
mariners wanted to save themselves. They decided
to do what Jonah suggested; they threw him into
the sea.

What would we do if faced with such a situation?
Would we take one person who confessed to being
the cause of our distress and throw that person to
what we believed to be a sure death? If we were sure

that the person confessing was indeed the sacrifice necessary, we might consider one life for many.

Jonah needed to be isolated from the mariners so that God could talk with him. He had ignored God's instructions, and God used the storm to get his attention. God used the mariners as agents to get him off the ship and into isolation. Although the mariners did not know that Jonah would not perish in the storm, they threw him overboard. Fortunately for them, that act calmed the sea.

Is God trying to get our attention today? Are we traveling in a vehicle that we need to be thrown out of? Could it be a vehicle of career preoccupation or a vehicle of jealousy or even a vehicle of obsession with our children? Do we need to get out of the vehicle and spend some quality time alone with God? Jonah needed three days and nights. How much time do we need?

Lord, make me aware of my need to spend time alone with you. Don't let me be caught up in riding on a stormy sea. Amen.

WHAT SHALL WE RENDER?

MICAH 6

*He has told you, O mortal, what is good; and
what does the LORD require of you but to do
justice, and to love kindness, and to walk humbly
with your God? (Micah 6:8)*

What shall we render to God? What does he
want us to do? How can we please him? I suppose
these were the questions in the minds of the
Israelites. God had sent Micah to tell them of their
great sins and to remind them of the way they had
been delivered from bondage in Egypt, redeemed
from slavery, and saved through so many acts of
mercy. Did God expect them to bow down, to bring
burnt offerings, to present gifts of oil or offspring?

Micah made it clear that God had already told
them what was good. All God required was that

they do justice, love kindness, and walk humbly with him. Was that so hard? It probably was for the Israelites, for Micah had preached about their injustices. They had been cheating the poor, accepting bribes, and using their positions of power unfairly. They were not doing justice.

Neither did they love kindness. Could any of their misdeeds be considered kind? They had fought and oppressed other nations. They had forgotten all that God had done for them and their ancestors. They had stood by when the poor and the unfortunate had been robbed. They had not been kind.

And they had not walked humbly. The powerful had sought more power. They had proclaimed God to be with them and had believed that no harm could come to them (3:11b). They did not know the meaning of humility.

What shall we render? It is simple. We give to God by being just. We give to God by loving kindness. And we give to God by walking humbly in obedience to his commandments. Will we do that?

Lord, help me do justice, love kindness, and walk humbly with you. Amen.

USELESS PLOTTING

NAHUM 1

*Why do you plot against the LORD? He will make
an end; no adversary will rise up twice.
(Nahum 1:9)*

ahum tried to warn the cruel people of
Nineveh that God would not allow them to continue to plot against him. How could they even
dream that they could succeed in their schemes?
They would be punished; God would surely bring
an end to their adversarial acts.

Have you ever encountered people who are con-
sistently engaged in cruel scheming? They do not
believe that they will be caught; they get away with
one scheme, and they think that they will get away
with all of them. They need to be reminded that

God told Nineveh through Nahum that he would bring justice and that no enemy would rise up twice.

I wonder whether the embezzler believes that he or she will ever be caught. What about the student who cheats on an exam to get an A or the worker who defames a coworker's reputation so that he or she can get an undeserved promotion? These are all plots against the Lord; and just as he did with Nineveh, God will bring an end to them.

So why should we engage in cruel plots? Don't we know how useless it is? We must learn to trust God to work out the details of our lives. Our responsibility is to love him; to do his will, to follow his law, and to love our neighbors. If we spent our time doing these things, we would not have time for useless plotting. The people of Nineveh learned the hard way; let us be smarter than they were.

Lord, keep us free from useless plots. You are our Ruler; teach us to let you rule. Amen.

IDOLS OR GOD?

HABAKKUK 2:18-20

What use is an idol once its maker has shaped it—a cast image, a teacher of lies? For its maker trusts in what has been made, though the product is only an idol that cannot speak!
(Habakkuk 2:18)

Habakkuk was disgusted. He had been crying to God for help, but God was not listening. He complained that all sorts of evil deeds were taking place and that God was doing nothing about them. Habakkuk did not realize that he was the one chosen to respond to the evils of the day. God told him to write the vision, make it plain, and wait for it to come to pass.

So Habakkuk told the people of the many charges against them. He let them know how foolish they were to put their trust in idols. They had shaped and cast images and then put their trust in what they had made. There was no logic, no rhyme or reason, for their actions, for they knew their products could not even speak.

What kind of idols are we making? Might they be man-made cars that need constant cleaning, servicing, and care? Perhaps our idol is jewelry that must be protected in a safe or made to shine so that it can sparkle in all its beauty and be admired. Maybe it's our television, the computer, the Internet, or a cell phone that has our devotion. All are man-made items that cannot do anything for us without our intervention. If we are worshiping any of these things, we are giving them the glory that belongs to God alone.

Habakkuk told the people, "The LORD is in his holy temple; let all the earth keep silence before him!" (2:20). Then he prayed that the God of whom he stood in awe would make his works known. Even though God might have to show his wrath, Habakkuk knew that God was his strength and his salvation and worthy of praise.

I hope we will listen to Habakkuk and discard our idols and return our full praise to God. Is anyone reading the vision? Habakkuk has made it plain.

Lord, help me discard my idols and worship you alone. Amen.

HIDING FROM GOD'S WRATH

ZEPHANIAH 2:1-4

Seek the LORD, all you humble of the land, who do his commands; seek righteousness, seek humility; perhaps you may be hidden on the day of the LORD's wrath. (Zephaniah 2:3)

I remember disobeying my mother when I was about six years old. I knew that my mother was going to punish me, so I tried to hide from her. I chose to hide, of all places, under the kitchen table. Somehow I thought the table would protect me, but it did not. Like the people of Judah, I should have been listening to Zephaniah's prophecy. Perhaps if I had appealed to my mother, obeyed her instructions, and tried to be the good child she expected, I could have been hidden from her anger. Of course, I was not humble, I was openly disobedient, I was tired of being good, and I was foolish enough to believe that a table could hide me.

It was Zephaniah's responsibility to deliver God's angry message. God promised to "utterly sweep away everything from the face of the earth" (1:2). God would search Jerusalem for those who had failed to obey his law, and he would punish them all. Nothing would save them. Their fine houses, great wealth, and vineyards would be of no use to them.

Zephaniah pleaded with the people to gather together and to seek the Lord, to seek righteousness and humility in hopes that they might avoid punishment. He knew that not everyone would do as he asked, but he thought that if even a few did what he suggested, those few might be hidden from God's wrath.

Are there those Christians with whom we can gather together and seek the Lord? Is there a group that desires to seek righteousness and humility? Is there a table under which we can hide until we have repented and been converted? Are we listening to Zephaniah?

Lord, prepare me to come out of hiding and to seek your righteousness. Amen.

GREATER THAN BEFORE
HAGGAI 2:1-9

The latter splendor of this house shall be greater than the former, says the LORD of hosts; and in this place I will give prosperity, says the LORD of hosts. (Haggai 2:9)

Although the Israelites had returned from exile in Babylon, they had not returned to God. They were not working to rebuild the temple in Jerusalem. They were still adjusting to being back home. God had to stir them out of their apathetic inactivity, and Haggai was sent with the message that God was with them and that God's house would be filled with glory.

Sometimes we, like the Israelites, are apathetic and inactive. We forget that God has all the silver and gold and that he can shake the heavens and the earth. How can we not serve him and build his house? We may be caught up in dreaming about the houses we can build and the money we can accumulate for ourselves, but we must remember that storms can destroy your houses and the stock market can claim our money. We are not in control.

Haggai told the Israelites not to be afraid, for greater things than they could even imagine would come to pass in God's new temple. They would be at peace, and God would be in his glory.

How can we build the temple for God? We can keep the temple of our bodies clean; we can bring disciples to our temple churches; we can give our time, talents, and resources to strengthen and restore the temples in which we worship. God is with us. We do not have to be apathetically inactive; neither do we have to be afraid!

Lord, I want to participate in building your temple. Use me in your service. Amen.

COME HOME

ZECHARIAH 1:1-6

Therefore say to them, Thus says the LORD of hosts: Return to me, says the LORD of hosts, and I will return to you, says the LORD of hosts.
(Zechariah 1:3)

In modern times, many young people who leave home to go to college or to get married return home after a few years. We call them boomerang kids. We throw them out there in the world, but they have difficulty making it on their own, and they return. We as parents may not have equipped them with the tools and skills they need to be successful in the world. They may be the type of young people who need more time at home, more love, more religious instruction, and even more discipline.

Just like our children, the Israelites had left home. They had been exiled—away from home, away from God, away from worship—so long that they had forgotten much of what their ancestors had taught. They did not remember what God had brought them through. They no longer had a temple in which to worship. They were preoccupied with their own dwelling places.

But God was faithful. God sent out a call for them to return home. In returning to Jerusalem, they were also supposed to return to God; however, they were distracted. God did not give up on them. He sent his prophet Zechariah to call them home. He promised that he would return to them and that they would be blessed.

We can do the same thing. We can call our children home and prepare them to return to the world as strengthened children of God. Just as God promised to be with the Israelites, he will be with us and with our children.

Lord, if I am reluctant to call my children home, give me the strength and wisdom to do so, knowing that you are the parent to whom we can always return. Amen.

Do You Want an Overflowing Blessing?

Malachi 3

Bring the full tithe into the storehouse, so that there may be food in my house, and thus put me to the test, says the LORD of hosts; see if I will not open the windows of heaven for you and pour down for you an overflowing blessing.
(Malachi 3:10)

$\mathcal{M}$alachi continues his question-and-answer technique as he explains how God will purify the descendants of Israel. They will be refined "like gold and silver, until they present offerings to the LORD in righteousness" (3:3*b*). He tells them if they return to God, God will return to them. They ask how they can return. Malachi tells them that they are robbing God with poor tithes and offerings; they are presenting less than the full amount. And even though they are robbing God, they still expect God to bless them.

This seems to be our story. We rob God all the time. We present less than a full tithe of our money, time, and talent, and yet, we expect God to bless us abundantly. Malachi lets us know that we have to put God to the test by first bringing the full tithe into God's house and then waiting for the overflowing blessing. We must learn to trust God and see if he is not a God of his word.

Have you ever budgeted the money from your paycheck and decided that there was more month than money? If you have, what was the first thing you cut out? Was it food or clothing? Was it your house or car payment? Was it gasoline for your car or your household utilities? I'll bet it was your offering to God. You cut it down a little, deciding not to give the full tithe. You do not believe that God will come through and open up the windows of heaven to pour out an overflowing blessing. The next time you are in this situation, put God to the test. If you always are blessed to have enough money to meet your living expenses, go beyond the full tithe, and give God an offering. You will receive an overflowing blessing!

Lord, I promise to stop robbing you. I will bring you the full tithe. I want an overflowing blessing. Amen.

ARE YOU TEMPTED?

MATTHEW 4:1-11

Jesus said to him, "Away with you, Satan! for it is written, 'Worship the Lord your God, and serve only him.'" (Matthew 4:10)

*J*esus was tempted and tested, and we will be, too. Let us consider what tempted Jesus and relate those temptations to our own lives.

The first temptation was to turn the stones into bread. Jesus had been praying and fasting in the wilderness for forty days and nights, so we know that he was hungry. But to use his great power to satisfy his hunger would have been selfish. Jesus could not selfishly satisfy his own needs. The reward for enduring this earthly hunger was a cross, not bread. Jesus simply told Satan that man does not live by bread alone.

The second temptation was to leap from the pinnacle of the temple and survive unharmed. This would have been a spectacular, sensational feat, but Jesus was not about the spectacular. He told Satan that we should not put God to the test.

The third temptation was to worship the tempter, and Jesus told Satan that we should fear and serve God and swear by his name. Jesus told Satan to get away, for there would be no bribes, sensations, or compromises.

What about us? How often do we use all we possess to satisfy selfish desires? We overspend our budgets on things we do not need, and we eat more food than our bodies can digest; yet, when we are asked to contribute to the poor and needy, we do not have sufficient funds. We would love to perform a sensational or spectacular act, would like our fifteen minutes of fame, and I am not sure we could resist if the opportunity presented itself. And we worship other gods. We are so much like the Israelites who had to be reclaimed year after year.

We are tempted and tested daily. What temptation or test can you resist today?

Lord, I need Jesus to walk with me today so that I can bravely resist the tests and temptations that I will face. Amen.

❧

ARE YOU A PEACEMAKER?

MATTHEW 5:1-11

Blessed are the peacemakers, for they will be called children of God. (Matthew 5:9)

𝒯here are some people who seem to bring peace to every situation, and then there are those who always seem to be surrounded by confusion. Some people seem to be the storm centers of bitterness and strife. Whenever a controversy arises, they are in the middle of it. They are troublemakers, not peacemakers.

Peacemaking starts from within. A peacemaker settles the peace issue within first and then moves from that inner struggle to the outer struggles to help right relationships between others.

Troublemakers have not dealt successfully with their inner peace issues.

Peacemakers are those in whose presence bitterness and strife just cannot survive. They try to bridge the gulfs and gaps that exist between people; they try to heal the broken places in the lives of those with whom they come in contact. And as children of God, they try to sweeten the bitterness they find in the world.

The Hebrew word for peace, shalom, does not mean simply the absence of trouble and evil, but it also means the presence and enjoyment of good. When my greeting to you is "Shalom," I want you to enjoy good, not just to avoid evil. A peacemaker does not just love peace, but works to make peace.

The shalom that surrounds the peacemaker, the good that is wished for those he or she encounters, means that troubling issues are faced and conquered; they are not avoided. The peacemaker as a child of God helps make the world a better place by helping disagreeable people resolve their differences and embrace one another in brotherly and sisterly love. Are there any peacemakers in your midst? Are you one?

Help me, Father, as one of your children, consciously become a peacemaker. Amen.

DIVIDED LOYALTIES

MATTHEW 12:22-32

He knew what they were thinking and said to them, "Every kingdom divided against itself is laid waste, and no city or house divided against itself will stand." (Matthew 12:25)

*J*esus cured a demoniac who was blind and mute. As the crowd noticed that the demoniac could see and speak, they wondered how Jesus was able to perform such miracles. Some thought he might be the Son of David, but others insisted that he had to be casting out demons in the name of the ruler of demons, Satan.

Jesus explained that no kingdom, city, or house divided against itself could stand. If he were casting out demons in the name of Satan, then he would be working against the very same Satan that he represented. That would destroy Satan's kingdom. However, if he were casting these demons out in the Spirit of God, then God would be present with them. To further illustrate his point, Jesus told them that before they could plunder a strong man's house, they would have to tie him up.

Kingdoms, cities, and houses cannot endure divided loyalties. Everyone concerned must declare his or her loyalty. Jesus said, "Whoever is not with me is against me, and whoever does not gather with me scatters" (12:30). How true this is. We all must work together to accomplish our goals. Whether we are engaged in some project for our nation, city, or home, we need everyone to be on the same page. We must join forces so that our efforts are strengthened, not sabotaged.

Have you ever discovered that someone who you thought was working for you was working against you? If you have, you must do what Jesus did. You must clear the air and make sure that your intentions are known. Once goals and objectives are clarified, each person can decide on their loyalty. Knowing where each person stands makes it easy to determine how to proceed. We, like Joshua, must decide whom we will serve. Do we represent Satan or the Spirit of God?

Lord, help me be loyal to you alone. Amen.

❧

WHAT COMES OUT OF YOUR MOUTH?

MATTHEW 15:10-20

It is not what goes into the mouth that defiles a person, but it is what comes out of the mouth that defiles. (Matthew 15:11)

*J*esus and the Pharisees clashed over their views of religion and God's requirements. The Pharisees were strict adherents of the Law of Moses, and they believed that Jesus instituted a new law. Jesus let them know that he was not changing the law but presenting a new interpretation of it.

The Pharisees concentrated on the external law that stated one had to wash in order to be clean, but Jesus' disciples ate without washing first. The internal law that Jesus brought recognized that cleanliness comes from within. It is what one is as opposed to what one does that makes one clean.

The Pharisees did not understand the difference between clean and unclean. The clean are those who are ready to worship God with their hearts, and the unclean are not ready because of what is in their hearts. So it is what comes out, not what goes in, that defiles.

What is it that comes out of our mouths? Are we so busy washing the outside and examining the food we consume that we fail to consider our words? Are we preparing our bodies and not our hearts to worship God? Do we pay attention to our words of worship, as well as our words of service?

We all know that words, once spoken, cannot be retracted. What if a person came to church in clothes that were not clean and felt uncomfortable because he or she could hear or sense the unkind words that were being spoken? Those who spoke the unkind words or communicated unwelcoming vibes were not clean people prepared to worship. They may have been clean on the outside, but their hearts were unclean.

Let today be the day that you carefully consider every word that comes out of your mouth. Your mother probably told you not to say anything if you could not say something good. Take that a step further; don't even think anything that is not good. Clean up your heart.

Lord, give me a clean heart that I may serve you. Amen.

❧

What Do You Say?

Matthew 16:13-20

He said to them, "But who do you say that I am?"
(Matthew 16:15)

$\mathcal{H}$ow long does it take for someone to really know who you are? Can we get to know another person in a week, a month, a year, or ever? Stories of how couples met and how long it took before they knew each other well enough to know that this was the person they wanted to marry always fascinate me. Marriage is a lifetime commitment, and one would certainly want to know the person he or she was marrying pretty well. Of course, some people tell us that we never really know another person.

If we were asked the question, "Who do you say that I am?" by your spouse, a family member, or a friend, what would you say? Do you know that person well enough to give a truthful answer, and is the answer that you would give different from the one someone else would give?

Jesus felt that he had been with the disciples long enough for them to discover his true identity. He asked them what others were saying. Who did the people in the street think that he was? Several different answers were given. Some thought that he was Elijah or John the Baptist or Jeremiah or one of the prophets. Although Jesus listened to these answers, he wanted to know what his disciples thought. After all, they were the ones who had traveled with him, lived with him, and eaten with him. What did they really think about his identity?

It is not surprising that Peter would be the one to answer this question. Peter was the bold one, the one who had asked to walk on water. Peter had to know who Jesus really was. Peter had been with him from the beginning. He and his brother were the first disciples chosen. If he did not know Jesus, who did? Peter did not disappoint Jesus in his answer, for Peter proclaimed that Jesus was the Christ, the Son of the Living God.

Peter's was a personal answer, and yours must be personal, too. Who do you say Jesus is? Is he your Christ, Son of the Living God?

Lord, with Peter I boldly proclaim you to be the Christ! Amen.

122

YOU SHOULD HAVE BEEN HERE

MATTHEW 20:1-16

*And about five o'clock he went out and found
others standing around; and he said to them,
"Why are you standing here idle all day?"
(Matthew 20:6)*

$\mathcal{J}$esus tells the story of laborers who had been
hired to work in the vineyard. After agreeing to a
fair wage for a day's work, they began to work early
in the morning. Later, other laborers were hired,
and later, still more were hired. Those who had
been hired first, borne the heat of the day, and done
the most work felt that they should have been paid
the most. Those laborers were thinking only of the
physical work they had done. They did not think
about the preciousness of the time shared with
other workers. They did not think of the joy that
comes from doing good work and from helping to

cultivate a vineyard. They thought only of the discomfort of the burning sun, and they knew that they deserved more than the latecomers.

How like the first laborers we are! We hate to see those who have been recently hired promoted to positions when those in long-standing with the company are overlooked. We don't consider how much the newcomers missed in not growing with the company and sharing in failures and successes. We don't think of saying, "You should have been here!"

Although the latecomers to the vineyard missed the fellowship and joy of having work to do all day long, they did not miss the monetary reward. They earned the same money that the first laborers earned. That is another problem that we often face. Why are those who are hired last paid more? We might be told that the fair market value has increased since we were hired; yet, how does one put a price tag on experience? These latecomers have missed the experiences we have shared and from which we have grown. They should have been here.

Jesus has told us that the first shall be last and the last shall be first in several ways. Time served is not important, but faithfully completing our tasks is. If we are blessed to serve a long time, we can say to the latecomers, "You should have been here!"

Lord, whether last or first, I just want to be included in the Kingdom. Amen.

❧

SYMBOL OF DENIAL

MATTHEW 26:69-75

*Then he began to curse, and he swore an oath,
"I do not know the man!" At that moment the
cock crowed. (Matthew 26:74)*

During a vacation in Europe, I noticed a statue of a rooster on top of several churches. When I asked about its being there, I was told that the rooster is a reminder that we may claim to be Christian and believers in Jesus, but we, like Peter, often deny that we know the Master. I have even begun to see rooster pins and necklaces in Christian gift shops. I suppose the feeling is that we need to remember not to deny Jesus.

Although I bought a rooster pin, I always wear it with a cross. The cross symbolizes my faith, but the rooster symbolizes my weakness. Peter is not alone in his denial. We all deny Jesus. We deny him when we fail to witness to doubting neighbors; we deny him when we fail to obey the commandments; and we deny him when we fail to study his word. There are so many ways that we deny him.

Peter had boldly claimed that he would never deny Jesus. When Jesus informed the disciples that they would all become deserters, Peter said, "Though all become deserters because of you, I will never desert you" (26:33). Even after Jesus responded that Peter would deny him three times before the cock crowed, Peter still insisted, "Even though I must die with you, I will not deny you" (26:35).

Oh how disappointed Peter was in himself when the cock crowed. He remembered Jesus' words, and he wept bitterly. Perhaps if we wear that symbol of denial, that rooster, we will remember never to deny Jesus. Then we will not have to weep.

Lord, help me to be faithful to my promise never to deny you. I really do not want to hear the cock crow. Amen.

HE IS NOT HERE

MATTHEW 28:1-15

He is not here; for he has been raised, as he said. Come, see the place where he lay. (Matthew 28:6)

The most meaningful part of my trip to the Holy Land was my visit to the Garden Tomb. Although it is not known that the place I visited was the actual place Jesus was laid, it was close enough for me.

I saw a stone like the one that had been rolled away. I climbed into the tomb and felt the stone slab on which a body could have lain, and as I turned to climb out, I noticed the sign just above the exit. It said, "He is not here; he is risen." At that moment I said to myself, "Of course he is not here, for if he were here or if there were some bones here, my faith is in vain." I know that the resurrection is the essential Christian truth. If we as Christians do not believe that he was raised, then we might as well claim another faith.

The chief priests and the Pharisees were so afraid that Jesus would be raised that they sought to seal the tomb. They posted guards and then paid them to say that while they were asleep the disciples had stolen Jesus' body. They could not allow people to remember that Jesus had told them that he would rise on the third day.

I often teach a class on comparative religions, and at the end of the class I ask students to discuss the religion that has had the most meaning for them. One young woman said that she is a Christian because Buddha lived, taught his Eightfold Noble Path, died, and is still dead. Muhammad lived; established a new culture; introduced the teachings of the Koran, the Articles of Belief, and The Five Pillars; died; and is still dead. But Jesus lived, brought the Good News, died, and got up! He is risen, as he said!

All the other great religious leaders are still dead. We can visit their graves and be assured that their remains are still there. But Jesus, my Savior, is not in the tomb. He is God with us. He got up! Praise be to God!

Father, you gave us your Son so that we might have eternal life. Thank you. Amen.

❧

SABBATH DEEDS

MARK 3:1-6

Then he said to them, "Is it lawful to do good or to do harm on the sabbath, to save life or to kill?" But they were silent. (Mark 3:4)

What do you do on the Sabbath or the day you observe as your Sabbath? Like most Christians, I observe Sunday, the Lord's Day, as my Sabbath. I know that the Sabbath is the seventh day of the week, the day on which God rested from his labors. But my Lord and Savior rose on Sunday, the first day of the week. From that first resurrection, the Lord's Day has been the Sabbath that many Christians observe.

But how do we observe it? I remember that as a child, I was not allowed to wash, iron, or go to the movies on Sunday. After Sunday school and church service, I read or studied and reflected on the week ahead. I find it difficult to break those observances as an adult.

Earnestly seeking to discredit Jesus and his ministry, the Pharisees attacked him regarding the observance of the Sabbath. They knew that he allowed his disciples to pluck grain on the Sabbath, and they waited to see whether he would heal a man with a withered hand on the Sabbath right in the synagogue. Jesus knew that they were testing him, so he asked them if it was lawful to do good or to do harm on the Sabbath, to save life or to kill. They could not answer him, and he healed the man's withered hand. After this healing, the Pharisees conspired to destroy Jesus.

We are not challenged to do good deeds on the Sabbath the way that Jesus was. No one will seek to destroy us if we do good deeds on the day we observe the Sabbath. Many of us do the same things on our Sabbath that we do every other day of the week. Often there is no special time set apart to worship God, not even to attend church. There are no acts considered to be too mundane to be performed on the Sabbath.

What if we were to vow to do only good deeds on the Sabbath or the Lord's Day? Could we restore the type of observance God intended?

Lord, I vow to monitor my Sabbath deeds. Amen.

❧

ONLY THROUGH PRAYER

MARK 9:14-29

He said to them, "This kind can come out only through prayer." (Mark 9:29)

A distressed father brought his spirit-possessed son to Jesus' disciples, hoping that they might cast the spirit out. But they could not, so the father brought his son to Jesus. I am sure that he reasoned that if the followers could not cast out the spirit, perhaps the leader could. When he explained that the disciples had failed, Jesus was greatly disturbed. Why had the disciples not learned to pray in faith, believing that what they asked for would be granted? How much longer would he be available to teach them?

The spirit-possessed boy fell on the ground and

rolled about, foaming at the mouth when the spirit saw Jesus. The spirit must have sensed that Jesus would pray, and prayer is the one thing that evil spirits cannot endure. Jesus asked the father how long his son had been suffering like this, and the father responded, "From childhood." The father asked Jesus to help his son if he was able. Jesus let him know that he was able because all things are possible for one who believes.

Jesus commanded the unclean spirit to come out of the boy, and it convulsed him so badly that all who were present believed the boy was dead. But Jesus took his hand and revived him. Of course the disciples wanted to know why they could not cast out the spirit, and Jesus let them know that they had not prayed in faith.

What is it that we cannot accomplish because we do not pray in faith? Is there a goal that you have set for yourself but fail to believe you will ever achieve? If there is, consider whether you have prayed in faith. Those who pray and believe can accomplish far more than had ever been conceived. If you are facing a really tough problem, you need to turn it over to God in prayer. The only way some problems are solved is through prayer.

Lord, give me the wisdom to turn my problems over to you and pray, knowing that they will be solved. I claim the victory today. Amen.

❧

ASKING FOR TOO MUCH

MARK 10:35-45

*James and John, the sons of Zebedee, came for-
ward to him and said to him, "Teacher, we want
you to do for us whatever we ask of you."*
(Mark 10:35)

*J*ames and John approached Jesus with what
seems to have been an outrageous request. They
actually asked Jesus to do whatever they asked.
They could have asked for some destructive act of
nature to occur or for someone to be killed or to
have riches untold, but they asked to have elevated
positions in the Kingdom. Just asking for that vio-
lated so much of what Jesus had taught in the
Sermon on the Mount. Didn't they remember that
the meek, the poor in spirit, and the peacemakers
are blessed? Their request did not place them
among the blessed.

How did Jesus respond to their bold request? Jesus told them that they did not know what they were asking. What he had to do required suffering, and he wanted to know if they were able to suffer with him. They said that they were, but they did not know what they would have to endure. Jesus let them know that he could not grant their request, for it was not his to grant. Their very request caused unrest among the other disciples, and Jesus had to reprimand them for seeking to be elevated. He told them that whoever wanted to be great must be the servant of all.

We may desire greatness. We want to plan our time of fame precisely. We do not want to serve; we want to be served. No one wants to be last; we all want to be first. We want to define our greatness.

The Christian cannot do that. The Christian, as a follower of Jesus, must be willing to serve without regard for position or cost. The Christian must be willing to take a backseat or perhaps no seat at all so that the needs of others can be met.

What high position or place of honor are you seeking? Are you able to endure the suffering and bear the pain that accompany it?

Lord, just allow me to be one of your faithful servants. My elevation will come, as I am welcomed into the Kingdom. Amen.

YOUR BROTHER HAS COME

LUKE 15:11-32

He replied, "Your brother has come, and your father has killed the fatted calf, because he has got him back safe and sound." (Luke 15:27)

$\mathcal{C}$an you just imagine the response of the prodigal's brother? He has been working all day and returns home to find all the lamps burning and music playing. There is even dancing and singing. What is going on? Why all the fun? Is it a party? When he asks these questions, he is told, "Your brother has come."

Then I am sure that this prodigal's brother asks himself some questions. I believe he asks, "Is it the brother that has squandered our father's wealth in loose living? Is it the brother from whom we have not heard until he had run out of money and friends? Is it the brother who played while I worked in the fields? What brother?" He has not seen his brother; in fact, he no longer thinks he has a brother. Yet, their father has chosen to honor that brother.

This prodigal's brother may reflect our response. We, too, would have been hurt. We might have refused to attend the party. We would have wondered how our father could be so unfair as to honor one who had thrown away so much. We would not think about what we enjoy every day of our lives. We would have forgotten that this brother is a son whom our father loves.

Are we jealous of those who repent and share the blessings for which we have not ceased to work? Are we just a little self-righteous, believing that we have no need for repentance? Think about it. God's love and blessings are more than sufficient for both the sinner who repents and returns to the fold and also the sinner who never left the fold.

Father, thank you for loving and accepting me as a member of your family, no matter where I have wandered. Amen.

HE WAS SHORT

LUKE 19:1-10

He was trying to see who Jesus was, but on account of the crowd he could not, because he was short in stature. (Luke 19:3)

$\mathcal{I}$ come from a family of short people. My mother is only four feet ten inches, and my father was only five feet seven inches. I always wanted to be tall, so I guess I did the next best thing by marrying a man who is six feet five inches. I can easily understand how Zacchaeus felt when he could not see Jesus over the crowd. Many times when my husband and I are in a crowd, he will say smugly, "I know you can't see because you are too short."

But Zacchaeus did not allow his stature to deter him. He ran ahead of the crowd and climbed a tree.

He could not add inches to his physical frame, so he added inches by using nature. How very clever of him! He found a way to see Jesus. By placing himself in such a prominent position it was easy for Jesus to see and inform Zacchaeus that he was going home with him. It is interesting to note that Jesus said, "I must stay at your house today." Jesus did not say that he wanted to stay there but that he had to stay there.

Jesus had a special purpose for staying with Zacchaeus. Many in the crowd grumbled because they felt that Zacchaeus was a sinner and was not worthy of Jesus' company. But Jesus proved them wrong. While Jesus stayed at his house, Zacchaeus was converted. Zacchaeus pledged to give half of his possessions to the poor and to quadruple any amount that he had taken unfairly. Jesus brought salvation to Zacchaeus's house because Zacchaeus was worthy.

Jesus came to save sinners and to call them into repentance. We must join in this effort, for we cannot save those with whom we do not come in contact. All are worthy of salvation. If we are too mentally short to see this, perhaps we need to climb a tree.

Lord, increase my mental stature so that I freely will reach out to all people, regardless of their status in life, and tell them about Jesus. Amen.

❧

WINE FOR A WEDDING

JOHN 2:1-12

*When the wine gave out, the mother of Jesus said
to him, "They have no wine." (John 2:3)*

I visited Cana when I went to the Holy Land,
and there was a church erected on the spot identified
as the place where the famous wedding at Cana
occurred. Of course, there was also a store across the
street from the church where one could buy wine
claimed to be the best in the world. How interesting it
was to walk out of a church and buy wine. My entire
tour group wanted to take some of the wine from
Cana home with them because the turning of water
into wine was the first miracle Jesus performed.

Let's look at the circumstances surrounding that first miracle. We find Jesus and his mother and other friends enjoying the wedding festivities when the wine runs out. It must have been most embarrassing for the wedding planners. Some scholars even believe that Mary, Jesus' mother, might have been one of those planners, which explains why she told Jesus about the situation. She knew that whatever the problem, he could fix it.

Perhaps Jesus was not yet ready to begin his miracle ministry, but his mother knew that it was time. Even after he said to her, "Woman, what concern is that to you and to me? My hour has not yet come" (2:4), she simply told the servants to do whatever he told them to do. There was no more discussion, for Jesus proceeded to tell the servants to fill the six twenty- or thirty-gallon jars with water. Jesus made sure that this time they would not run out.

Wine is recognized as an enhancer to food and to life. It brings a good feeling and outlook for the future. That, of course, is what is desired at a wedding. We want the food to taste good, and we want a happy future for the couple. Jesus, like fine wine, enhances life and gives those who partake of him a good feeling and outlook for the future.

Lord, I want to enjoy the fine wine of knowing you. Amen.

WHAT DO YOU WANT?

JOHN 5:1-18

When Jesus saw him lying there and knew that he had been there a long time, he said to him, "Do you want to be made well?" (John 5:6)

$\mathcal{I}$ can't imagine lying beside a pool for thirty-eight years; yet, there was a paralyzed man who had been lying beside the pool of Bethzatha for just that long. There were many invalids lying beside that pool, for they knew that once a year the water in the pool was stirred, and the first one in the pool was healed of his or her infirmities.

In thirty-eight years, couldn't this man have managed to be the first one in the pool? He claimed that he had no one to put him in the water and that

141

someone else always got there first. He made excuses, but Jesus wanted to know if this man really wanted to be made well. Jesus knew that sometimes an excuse masks half-hearted dedication to be healed.

Somehow, even though he never answered Jesus' question, the man must have convinced Jesus that he did want to be well because Jesus commanded him to take up his bed and walk. The healing was immediate. Thirty-eight years of suffering were gone in an instant. Jesus spoke life into the man's paralyzed limbs.

Sometimes we are in situations that paralyze us. We cannot move out of the state we find ourselves in. We keep waiting for someone to help us or take us to the place where relief is possible. If no one offers, we continue to sit and wait. But Jesus asks us if we want to be well. Do we want our situation to improve, or are we too apathetic to do anything about it? Perhaps we, too, will just lie around for thirty-eight years.

Every day Jesus is available to stir the waters of our lives. All we need to do is have faith that our situations can change. Once we have claimed our way out, we are empowered to move toward it. What do you want? Stop making excuses, and claim it!

Lord, move me toward wholeness by claiming my victory with you. Amen.

A PLACE PREPARED

JOHN 14:1-14

In my Father's house there are many dwelling places. If it were not so, would I have told you that I go to prepare a place for you? (John 14:2)

Have you ever checked in at a hotel and discovered that the room you reserved was not available? Housekeeping was running behind, and it would be quite a while before your room was properly prepared. Were you angry or at least disappointed because you had been traveling and were looking forward to getting in your room and relaxing before your next appointment? Your place was not prepared.

Jesus was preparing the disciples for his death, and he told them about the place he was going. It was to his Father's house where there were many dwelling places. He was going ahead of them so that he would have time to prepare a place for them. They would not have to arrive and find that their place was not prepared.

What do we have to do to be ready to dwell in the place that Jesus is preparing? I remember hearing some older mothers of the church proclaim that they were sending up their timber, and I wondered what they were talking about. Then I read this scripture, and I knew that they were sending necessary supplies to heaven so that they would be sure to have a place prepared.

What kind of timber are you sending up? Those church mothers meant that they were doing deeds of kindness and were saying their prayers and reading their Bibles. They also were attending worship and visiting the sick and shut in, and they were living within the love of God. They knew what Jesus had said; he was preparing a place for them. They believed him because he said, "If it were not so, would I have told you that I go to prepare a place for you?" By sending up their timber, they were making sure that their place would be ready when they arrived.

Help me, Lord, to send up my timber so that I can dwell in the place that you have prepared. Amen.

THE ANNOUNCEMENT

JOHN 20:1-18

Mary Magdalene went and announced to the disciples, "I have seen the Lord"; and she told them that he had said these things to her.
(John 20:18)

When Mary Magdalene made the announcement, "I have seen the Lord," she became the first postresurrection preacher of the gospel. What a glorious thing to be able to announce that you have seen the Lord, and your life ought to witness to that fact.

How was Mary prepared to make her announcement? First, she was exorcised of her demons. What are the demons that dwell within us? Are they power, greed, jealousy, and wealth? How do we rid ourselves of them? We, like Mary, have to go to Jesus and allow him to exorcise them from us. We must honestly desire to be released from our need for power or wealth and from our spirit of jealousy and greed. There are so many more demons that may possess us, but if we are to make the announcement, they must go.

Second, we must be out front in our service. Every time the little band of women who followed Jesus is named, Mary Magdalene's name heads the list. She was a leader, and she gave of her own resources to support Jesus' ministry. If we are to make the announcement, we must follow Mary's example.

Third, we must be patient in our waiting. Mary Magdalene was the last one at the cross and the first one at the tomb. Her demons no longer plagued her, so she had the ability to wait. We often cannot wait for something because our demons control us. We are in a hurry to gain power and wealth and to have all that the Joneses have. There is no way we can wait for the Lord to reveal himself to us. But if we don't wait, if we leave like Peter and John did, we will not be able to make the announcement.

Fourth, we must be bold in our witness. Once we have seen the Lord, we must run and tell everybody. Have you seen him?

Lord, I want to make the announcement. I want to see you. Amen.

🐝

DO YOU LOVE ME MORE?

JOHN 21:1-19

When they had finished breakfast, Jesus said to Simon Peter, "Simon son of John, do you love me more than these?" He said to him, "Yes, Lord; you know that I love you." Jesus said to him, "Feed my lambs." (John 21:15)

a message often exchanged between lovers is, "I love you more than I did yesterday, but less than I will tomorrow." This message is shortened to "More than yesterday, less than tomorrow." What an awesome promise, but it was just the type of promise that Jesus was expecting of Peter.

After the resurrection, Jesus appeared several times. One of these times he found the disciples fishing. Although they had fished all night, they had not caught anything. After directed to cast their nets in a certain spot, they had more fish than they could haul in. Realizing who Jesus was, they went ashore and joined him for breakfast.

When breakfast was finished, Jesus directed his conversation to Peter. He wanted to know if Peter loved him more. We know that Peter boldly proclaimed that he would never deny Jesus, but three times he did. Jesus knew that he had repented of this denial, and he was giving Peter an opportunity to prove that he did, in fact, love him more. Peter knew that Jesus knew the extent of his love, but Peter had to verbalize it. Then that love had to be expressed by feeding the lambs, or the children who would become disciples. Jesus kept giving Peter opportunities to disavow his loyalty. He asked three times if Peter loved him, and each time Peter answered affirmatively. It was important that Peter be very clear about his feelings because he would be forced to go where he did not want to go and die a painful death. Being sure that Peter loved him more, Jesus told him, "Follow me."

Do we love Jesus more? Do we love our spouses more? Do we love our children and parents more? Who is it that we love more? Who is it that we would be willing to die for? To whom could we say, "More than yesterday, less than tomorrow"? Those we love, we must feed and nurture.

Lord Jesus, I love you, and I will feed your lambs. Amen.

HOW BOLD ARE YOU?

ACTS 3–4

Now when they saw the boldness of Peter and John and realized that they were uneducated and ordinary men, they were amazed and recognized them as companions of Jesus. (Acts 4:13)

a man, lame from birth, was brought to Peter and John as they entered the temple. He asked them for alms, but they had no money. They decided to give the man what they did have. They gave him the healing power of the name of Jesus. There were people around who heard and saw what had happened. They knew that Peter and John were not ashamed to have been with Jesus.

Peter used this opportunity to preach to the people who had gathered, and he told them how faith in the name of Jesus had made the lame man strong.

He charged them to repent, turn to God, and be forgiven of their sins. The Sadducees preached that there is resurrection of the dead in Jesus only, so Peter and John were arrested. But the next day they stood before the rulers and members of the high priestly family and boldly announced that they were able to do all that they did in the name of Jesus, for there was no other name by which we are saved.

There was no way to dispute what Peter and John were saying because the lame man was standing before them, and the people had seen the healing occur. There was no other explanation. They were just ordinary men, but they were bold in proclaiming their faith. They had to have been companions of Jesus.

What about you and me? Can anyone recognize us as companions of Jesus? Are we bold in our witness and in our calling others to repentance? Would we risk imprisonment for proclaiming that the name of Jesus is the only one that saves us? When the high rulers saw the boldness of Peter and John, they knew the two had been with Jesus. Who have we been with? How bold are we?

Lord, give me the faith to witness boldly in the name of Jesus. Amen.

COMING AND GOING
THE SAME WAY

ACTS 16:16-40

*But Paul replied, "They have beaten us in public,
uncondemned, men who are Roman citizens, and
have thrown us into prison; and now are they
going to discharge us in secret? Certainly not! Let
them come and take us out themselves."*
(Acts 16:37)

Some people are very superstitious about
entering and leaving through the same door. There
is something about maintaining order and clear
paths in life. Well, Paul and Silas had been beaten in
public and thrown into prison after they had
ordered the spirit of divination out of a slave girl.
The girl had used this spirit to tell fortunes, and her
owners had made a good deal of money because of
her spirit. When Paul ordered the spirit out of the

girl, the owners' source of easy income was gone.

Of course, Paul and Silas were not distraught by their fate. They had a worship service while in prison. They prayed and sang hymns, and God heard them. God caused an earthquake, which loosened their chains and opened their cell doors. They were free to go, but they did not leave. When the jailer woke up, he started to kill himself, for he knew that he had not kept his prisoners in jail. But Paul told him not to harm himself because they all were there. Realizing that the religion Paul and Silas preached had to be more powerful than anything he had ever experienced, the jailer asked what he had to do to be saved. The jailer and his household were baptized, and they all fellowshipped with Paul and Silas in the jailer's house.

The next morning, after word had spread about what had happened, the magistrates sent the police to tell the jailer to let Paul and Silas go. Paul and Silas believed in coming and going the same way. They had been imprisoned in public, beaten in public, and brought before the magistrates. They wanted to be dismissed before the magistrates, and they, as Roman citizens, wanted an apology for their imprisonment. The magistrates were afraid of these powerful men of God, and they did what was requested.

Lord, give us the wisdom to ask for respect even from authorities. Our lives are always in order when we come and go with you. Amen.

Justified by Faith

Romans 3:21-31

*For we hold that a person is justified by faith
apart from works prescribed by the law.
(Romans 3:28)*

It was while Martin Luther was reading Paul's epistle to the Romans that he realized that we are justified by faith, not by works. At the time of this revelation, the Pope was sending his agent to sell indulgences for sin. It was believed that some people had more than enough good works to get them into heaven and that some of their good works could be sold to others.

I can imagine that Martin Luther was thinking of someone like Martha, a woman who had always been a faithful church worker. Martha was at the church each time the doors were opened; she helped prepare meals for the sick and shut-in, prepared the communion table, taught a Bible study, and sang in the choir. Surely she had an abundance of good works. Now compare her to Sally who rarely came to church and never did any service. Did the Pope believe that Sally could buy some of Martha's good works? Martin Luther proclaimed that he did not believe it. He said that we are justified by faith and that good works don't make us good, but good people do good works.

I wonder when we will learn that lesson. Many of us are busy trying to do enough good works to make up for the multitude of sins that we commit daily. We do not realize that we are working on the wrong thing. None of us is righteous, and no matter how many good works we do, we never will be righteous. We need to work on our faith and commitment to God. God has extended grace to us. There is nothing we can do to earn it.

Jesus has paid the price. We owe our salvation to him, and that salvation is extended to all who believe. The law is our guide, and it is a law of faith: "For we hold that a person is justified by faith apart from works prescribed by the law" (3:28). Those who, by faith, abide by the law will do good works.

Father, increase my faith so that my good works are automatic. Amen.

RUNNING TO WIN

1 CORINTHIANS 9:24-27

*Do you not know that in a race the runners all
compete, but only one receives the prize? Run in
such a way that you may win it.*
(1 Corinthians 9:24)

ave you ever thought about the vast numbers of hours spent in preparing for a race? Each runner is trained extensively and is told to focus on his or her own lane. They are told not to worry about the other runners; their only concern should be to honor the personal goals they have set for themselves. The one who has worked the hardest, has the greatest desire to win, and has set his or her personal goals the highest will win the prize.

There have been many runners who have followed this advice. Consider Gail Devers, who overcame Graves' disease, bleeding feet, and threatened amputation to win her race. Then there was Gwen Torrence, who came back from time off for childbirth to win her race. And we cannot forget Wilma Rudolph, who overcame polio as a child to win her races. They kept their eye on the prize, and they won.

What is it that we want to win? What is the prize that we feel we must have? For some of us, it may be wealth or a high-powered job or a beautiful house. For others it may be as simple as being a part of a family with devoted parents and happy children. But what is the prize that Paul challenged the church at Corinth to win? Paul wrote to the Corinthians about his many experiences and encounters with Jews and Gentiles. He had learned to associate with everyone so that he could win souls for Christ. He said, "I have become all things to all people, that I might by all means save some" (9:22b). The prize he sought was sharing in the blessings of the gospel. He understood that by living according to the high calling of Christ, he ultimately would abide with Christ in heaven.

I wonder whether we are willing to accept Paul's challenge. Can we associate with those who do not meet our social, educational, and financial standards? Are we willing to go to the shelters and the sons to win souls for Christ? Are we running this e of life to win eternal life?

Lord, I am running, trying to make heaven my home. Amen.

STRENGTH IN WEAKNESS

2 CORINTHIANS 12

Therefore I am content with weaknesses, insults, hardships, persecutions, and calamities for the sake of Christ; for whenever I am weak, then I am strong. (2 Corinthians 12:10)

Paul wrote of his weaknesses. He had a thorn in the flesh that God would not remove. He had been beaten, stoned, shipwrecked, and imprisoned. He had been hungry, cold, and naked. He had worried about the churches so recently established; he considered himself to be weak. He accepted his thorn in the flesh because he knew that God's grace was sufficient. He grew to understand that God's power is made perfect in weakness. All that he suffered had made him strong.

Are we content with weakness? I know that I am not. I want to be good at what I do. I want to be strong for my family. I do not like to fail. I am not content when I suffer hardships and persecutions; yet, I do know that I have grown whenever I have suffered. When I was in school, I was challenged to achieve academic excellence because it was not believed that a black girl could do it. When I was in Corporate America, I was promoted to management even though I had to overcome racial and sexual barriers. I even became an award-winning author after receiving numerous rejection letters in response to the book that would win awards. Although I did not like them, the hardships made me strong.

What is your thorn in the flesh? What hardships and persecutions do you suffer? I am sure that you have not been beaten, stoned, shipwrecked, and imprisoned. You may not have been hungry, cold, and naked; but I know you have suffered because suffering is a part of life. How have you handled your weaknesses? Have you asked for your thorn to be removed, or have you received Paul's message that God's grace is sufficient?

I can testify that there is strength in weakness. God is in control of the lives that we submit to him. Let God lead you and make you strong.

Father, I surrender my life to you. Take my weaknesses, and make me strong. Amen.

THE ONLY THING THAT MATTERS

GALATIANS 5:2-6

For in Christ Jesus neither circumcision nor uncircumcision counts for anything; the only thing that counts is faith working through love.
(Galatians 5:6)

Some people are obsessed with keeping the law. The slightest infraction is severely punished. We all like to avoid people like that because we are painfully aware of the many times we break the law. We are quick to tell others how unimportant some laws are.

Paul warned the Galatians about their keeping part of the law but not all of it. Being circumcised was not the important thing. Circumcision was an external law. It even might have been done for show. Keeping the law could not earn salvation. It was the internal law; it was faith working in love that really mattered.

Faith works in love when we accept that person who does not have the same color skin we have. Faith works in love when we welcome the poorly dressed or homeless person into our churches and our homes. Faith works in love when we love God with all our hearts and minds and strength. Faith works in love when we love our neighbor as ourselves. We are saved by faith, and faith working in love is all that counts.

What external law do we keep while our faith fails to work in love? Think about it.

Lord, increase my faith and let it be evidenced in my works of love. Amen.

NO ROOM FOR THE DEVIL

EPHESIANS 4:25–5:2

And do not make room for the devil.
(Ephesians 4:27)

*T*here is a spiritual song that admonishes us to shut the door on the devil. I know that this is the sentiment of this verse in Ephesians that warns us not to make room for the devil. Both messages suggest that we are in control of our lives. We have the power to keep the devil out.

Let's look a little closer at the message to the Ephesians. In verse 25 of the fourth chapter, the Ephesians are advised not to lie. They are urged to speak truthfully to their neighbors because they all belong to one another. That seems to be good advice, for if we really considered others to be true neighbors and family members, they would expect us to be truthful.

Second, the Ephesians are told that when they are angry, they should not sin; they should never let the sun go down on their anger. This may be another way of telling them and us not to hold grudges. We may be angry for a time, but it is sinful to hold anger for several days. I am sure that we all know people who are still angry about something that happened forty years ago. That is sinful. Let your anger go; get over it. Anger that is held for days and years festers and causes health problems.

Third, the Ephesians are warned not to make room for the devil. We all know that the devil waits patiently to enter our lives. We need to have on the whole armor of God in order to withstand the wiles of the devil. Every day we are engaged in a battle to keep sin out of our lives, and we can win only if we put on Christ and keep lies and anger out. If we are filled with love, work hard, share with the needy, speak kindly to one another, and exercise forgiveness, we will become imitators of Christ. There will be no room for the devil. We can keep him out.

Father, help me follow this advice so wisely offered to the Ephesians. Amen.

❧❧

WHAT ARE YOU WEARING?

EPHESIANS 6:10-20

Put on the whole armor of God, so that you may
be able to stand against the wiles of the devil.
(Ephesians 6:11)

ow many times have you heard the question, "What are you wearing?" We all want to be properly dressed for every occasion. But are we properly dressed to stand firm in the face of evil? What is the proper attire to face the devil?

There is the belt of truth. This means that we should always be truthful. You probably were told not to tell lies because you would not be able to remember what you had said. You can always remember the truth. The belt of truth is part of the armor that will keep us from getting caught in the devil's web.

Then there is the breastplate of righteousness. We are shielded by what is right. When we live according to the laws of God, evil cannot penetrate our hearts. We will have to face evil, and it may hurt. But it will not penetrate and control our lives. The breastplate that we wear will be our protector, and we will be able to survive. The righteous God is our shield.

What kind of shoes should we wear? We will need to wear whatever makes us ready to proclaim the gospel of peace. We don't need to wear shoes that are too small or that hurt our feet because we will not be ready to proclaim the gospel of peace. We need to wear old, comfortable shoes—shoes that are familiar and comfortable with the gospel.

We also need to wear the shield of faith, which will enable us to stop the flaming arrows of evil. And on our heads, we need the helmet of salvation. We are saved by faith and covered from head to toe by God's armor. All we need is the sword of the spirit, which is the word of God. No evil scheme can harm us because we are wearing the right clothes. What are you wearing?

Lord, I want to be dressed in your whole armor, for when I face evil, I will be prepared for battle. Amen.

DOING ALL THINGS

PHILIPPIANS 4:4-14

I can do all things through him who strengthens me. (Philippians 4:13)

hat does it mean to have the confidence to do all things? Are there no exceptions? Looking at this chapter, we realize that Paul is sharing his past experiences with the church at Philippi, the church that he called his "joy and crown." He gives them the secret to having the confidence to do all things.

First, he tells them to rejoice in the Lord always. He urges them to be gentle to everyone and reminds them that the Lord is near. In order to be able to do all things, we must rejoice. It is a happy person, a rejoicing person, who is gentle and knows that God is near. And God enables that person to do all things.

Second, Paul tells them not to worry about anything: "But in everything by prayer and supplication with thanksgiving let your requests be made known to God" (4:6b). I have often heard, "If you are going to worry, don't pray." Paul is saying the same thing. We should not worry; we should spend our time in prayer. We make our requests to God, but we make those requests with thanksgiving. We must learn to stop praying those "gimme" prayers. We want God to give us this and give us that, but we never stop to thank God for what we already have. Perhaps if our prayers included more thanksgiving, there would be fewer requests.

Paul tells us to let the peace of God guard our hearts. And peace will do that when we concentrate and think on what is true, honorable, just, pure, pleasing, and commendable. With our minds thus occupied, the peace of God will be with us.

Having followed these instructions, we are ready to be content whether we are rich or poor or have little or plenty and no matter what circumstances we find ourselves in. Once we have learned this secret, we are confident that we can do all things through Christ who strengthens us.

Thank you, Lord, for giving me the power in Christ to do all things. Amen.

WISE COUNSEL

COLOSSIANS 4:2-6

Let your speech always be gracious, seasoned with salt, so that you may know how you ought to answer everyone. (Colossians 4:6)

*T*here is nothing worse than a person with a foul mouth. Parents used to wash their children's mouths out with soap when they uttered vulgar words or spoke in a disrespectful manner to their elders. I don't know of anyone who does that anymore, but it might not be a bad idea to start again.

What is gracious speech? How do we season it with salt? I suppose that gracious speech is polite speech. It is speech that makes the person being spoken to feel like a blessed child of God. It is probably speech that builds self-esteem and inspires trust. I know it is the way I would like to be spoken to.

This gracious speech is to be seasoned with salt. Salt adds flavor, so I suppose that speech seasoned with salt is interesting and enthusiastic. It is not boring, and it certainly does not put anyone to sleep. I remember telling my son to be enthusiastic and inspiring during a speech he delivered when he was running for student-body president of his high school. I told him that nobody wants a dull leader. When he was elected, the students believed that their high school was the greatest one in the world.

What if all of our speech was gracious and seasoned with salt? It would make life much more pleasant. I am sure that you have dealt with salespeople who were rude and abrupt. You have probably also dealt with service people who have made you feel as though they were doing you a favor when you were paying for their services. There was neither grace nor seasoning in their speech.

Paul wants the Colossians to be Christians who speak graciously and inspiringly to all they meet. Why don't we try to do that also?

Lord, season my gracious speech with salt. Amen.

GETTING EVEN

1 THESSALONIANS 5:12-15

See that none of you repays evil for evil, but always seek to do good to one another and to all. (1 Thessalonians 5:15)

$\mathcal{I}$ like to read the comic strip called "The Lockhorns." The strip features a husband and wife. The husband always gets drunk or in some other way is nonproductive, and the wife always goes to the beauty shop, talks on the phone, wrecks the car, and prepares poorly cooked meals. The Lockhorns are quite dysfunctional.

There was one strip in which Loretta, the wife, was waiting for her husband when he came home drunk. She took one look at him and said, "You know that man on my soap opera who looks just like you? Well, he got his today!" The implication was that her husband would get his, too! Loretta wanted him to know that his time was coming; he would have to pay for his sins.

Somehow, all of us expect the sins of others to catch up with them, but some of us are not willing to wait. We want to be the ones to make them pay for their sins. We want to repay evil for evil.

Paul spent most of his first letter to the Thessalonians encouraging them to live lives of holiness. He had given them hope in living and pleasing God. He wanted them to be able to live with God eternally in the heavens. So, he told them not to repay evil for evil, for repaying evil for evil was not their job. It was their job to do good works to and for one another.

What a wonderful blessing it would be if we could forget about getting even or repaying others for the evil they have done. God has promised to repay. Vengeance belongs to God. It is not ours. We have the power to repay evil with acts of kindness. We can pray for those who abuse and misuse us. We can overcome evil with good.

Lord, strengthen me to resist the urge to repay evil for evil. I know that I will be blessed as I seek to do good and kind acts for all of those with whom I come in contact. Amen.

Sound Advice

1 Thessalonians 5:16-28

Do not quench the Spirit. (1 Thessalonians 5:19)

𝒥 don't know how many times I heard as a child, "Do not quench the Spirit." I always wondered what "quench" meant, and the dictionary gives several definitions. It may mean to put out, as to extinguish; it may mean to bring to an end, as to overcome; or it may mean to repress or cool. So, what does it mean in the context of the Spirit? Let's take a closer look.

Paul ends his first letter to the Thessalonians with words of sound advice. He tells them to rejoice always and to pray without ceasing. The Spirit of God in us cannot be quenched, or put out, as long as we rejoice and pray. We quench the spirit when we cease to pray.

Next, Paul tells the Thessalonians to give thanks in all circumstances, knowing this is the will of God in Christ. If we were able to thank God no matter what our condition, we would not let the Spirit of God in us end. We could not overcome or quench it, for it would show forth in our lives.

Paul continues his advice by warning the Thessalonians not to despise the words of prophets, but to test everything and hold fast to what is good. The Spirit of God lives in us as it is bolstered by prophetic words. As we listen to the words of those claiming to be prophets, we must test their validity. We must hold on to the good and let go of the bad.

Last, Paul advises the Thessalonians to abstain from every form of evil. The Spirit of God cannot coexist with evil; the two are not compatible. So by allowing evil to rule our lives, we kill or quench the Spirit.

As a child, I suspected that quenching the Spirit had to do with people shouting or outwardly expressing their joy during worship. Some people tried to keep still or remain quiet when they wanted to shout. This also is a form of quenching the Spirit. When the Spirit of God moves within, respond. Do not quench it. That is sound advice.

Lord, I want your spirit to be visible in me. I will shout with joy! Amen.

❧

A WORTHY CALLING

2 THESSALONIANS 1:3-12

To this end we always pray for you, asking that our God will make you worthy of his call and will fulfill by his power every good resolve and work of faith. (2 Thessalonians 1:11)

What is a worthy calling? How does one know when he or she has truly been called of God? We currently have more than twenty persons in our church who have expressed a response to God's calling to the ministry. On the surface I can see that some are very sincere and committed to ministry, but others seem to be fascinated with what they feel will be the fame and glory of preaching. Of course, whether or not they are called is not for me to say. Only they and God know.

But if they are called, are they worthy of the call?

Paul expresses his concerns about the Thessalonians being worthy of God's calling. He is thankful that their faith is growing and that they are showing greater love for one another. He knows that they have been persecuted and afflicted, but they have endured. He is committed to praying for them and asking that God will make them worthy of his call to ministry and will empower them to fulfill every good resolve and work of faith.

Paul's words may embody our responsibility regarding those who would minister to us. We need to thank God for them and show our love toward them. We need to encourage them to endure hardships and remind them that God is strengthening them. We must above all else pray for them and ask God to make them worthy of his calling. Those who are worthy will have the God-given power to do good works.

So, rather than asking, "Who is worthy?" we need to ask, "What ministers or ministerial candidates do I need to be praying for?"

Lord, help me support those who are seeking to be worthy of their calling to your ministry. Amen.

HOMELESS RELATIVES

1 TIMOTHY 5:1-8

And whoever does not provide for relatives, and
especially for family members, has denied the
faith and is worse than an unbeliever.
(1 Timothy 5:8)

$\mathcal{G}$rowing up, I didn't see homeless people on
the streets. I know that everyone had relatives who
did not have their own homes, and those relatives
often lived with or rented rooms from the relatives
who did have homes. There was a cousin of my
mother's who lived with us for a short while. My
mother said that Cousin Bob was living with us
until he got on his feet. She said that he was having
a rough time and that we could not let him live on
the street.

Well, that sentiment has passed. There are so

many homeless people. Our streets and shelters are full. My church, Cascade United Methodist Church, operates a homeless shelter for men. We even conduct worship services at the shelter and arrange for the men to have physical and dental checkups and get hair cuts. But I often wonder where these men's relatives are. Doesn't anyone care that they have no place to live?

When I read the fifth chapter of 1 Timothy, I realized that it is a denial of faith to fail to provide for relatives. Why do we fail to provide for them? For one thing, we are unwilling to share our wealth. We feel that we have worked hard for what we have, and everyone else should do the same thing. Some believe that those we take into our homes, whether relatives or not, may steal our possessions, especially if they are on drugs. Some parents even have allowed their children to become homeless. The children had become abusive, and the parents could not take it anymore.

Why have we become a nation of homeless people? Don't we care that we are considered faithless and less than believers when we allow our relatives and family members to be homeless? Perhaps learning to respect our elders, caring for widows, and teaching our children their religious duties and responsibilities would lead us in the right direction.

Lord, open our hearts and homes to family members who need us. Amen.

❧

A LOVE AFFAIR WITH MONEY

1 TIMOTHY 6:3-10

*For the love of money is a root of all kinds of evil,
and in their eagerness to be rich some have
wandered away from the faith and pierced
themselves with many pains. (1 Timothy 6:10)*

*H*ave you ever wanted to have millions and
millions of dollars? Do you think about what you
would do with that much money and wonder what
people who have that much money do with it? I
have wondered about it, but I have not seriously
tried to do anything that would bring in that much
money. I just don't love money enough to do anything and everything to get it.

There are those who spend most of their pay-
checks buying lottery tickets. They imagine win-
ning millions and not having to work any more.

Then there are those who sell all that they have to buy stock in a company that they have heard is a hot commodity. There are those who bet on the outcome of sporting events, feeling confident that they have picked a winner. But the most distressing of all to me are those people who engage in the reality-television stunts to win a million dollars. They leave their families, eat rats, put the lives of others in jeopardy, and risk their own lives to be the lone survivor. Why?

I believe that Paul was thinking of such people when he wrote to Timothy. He was warning Timothy and his followers that "those who want to be rich fall into temptation and are trapped by many senseless and harmful desires that plunge people into ruin and destruction" (6:9). Whenever we are consumed by desire for riches, we lose our good sense and judgment. We fall victim to illegal and immoral schemes, and we forget that God has promised to provide for us. We destroy our families and ourselves when we greedily reach out for more than we need.

A Hindu belief is the path of desire is unfulfilling and contradictory, for worldly success is at best temporary. We know that we brought nothing into the world and can take nothing out of it (6:7).

Lord, keep me from a love affair with money. Amen.

❧

WORKING WITHOUT SHAME

2 TIMOTHY 2:14-19

*Do your best to present yourself to God as one
approved by him, a worker who has no need to be
ashamed, rightly explaining the word of truth.*
(2 Timothy 2:15)

*E*very time I teach a Bible study, I pray that I
will present myself as one approved by God, working without shame, and rightly explaining the word
of truth. I also pray for my students to show themselves approved, without shame, and able to explain
rightly the word of truth.

I find that so many who profess Christianity
know very little about the word of God. There are
some books of the Bible that they have never read
and never studied. They are long-term Christians,
but they have short-term knowledge.

We at my church seriously try to equip Christians to work without shame. We have more than fifty weekly Bible studies. We have periodic teacher training classes, and we constantly recruit those with the spiritual gift of teaching to stir up and use that gift.

I know that many professed Christians do not feel equipped to explain the word. They are ashamed of their meager knowledge, so they remain silent. They do not open the door to persons of other religious persuasions because they are not well-informed about their own. The solution is to study. With knowledge, there is no need to be embarrassed or ashamed.

I started reading the Bible from cover to cover when I was twelve years old. I rarely have missed reading a day since then. Of course, I have read the whole Bible many times, yet there is so much that I still have to learn. With each reading, a new perspective is gained. One of the true tests of Scripture is its timelessness; it is true and relevant for yesterday, today, and tomorrow. Study to show yourself approved unto God; be a person who works without shame and rightly explains the word of truth.

Lord, I promise to study so that I can work without shame for you. Amen.

❧

ARE YOU
A GOOD FIGHTER?

2 TIMOTHY 4:1-8

I have fought the good fight, I have finished the
race, I have kept the faith. (2 Timothy 4:7)

*D*o you remember the first fight you ever
had? Perhaps it was not your first fight, but it was a
childhood fight. I was never much of a fighter, but I
remember attempting to fight somebody for my sister. My sister was a pianist, and she did not want to
risk injuring her hands. So she called on me to fight
for her. I gathered my friends around me and went
to meet the girl my sister was scheduled to fight.
The fight never took place, for when that girl saw
my crowd of friends, she retreated. I always
believed that she thought my sister was in the

crowd and had gathered her friends to help her fight. Little did she know that my sister was at home practicing her piano lesson. She was not a good fighter because she allowed others to fight for her, and I was not a good fighter because I needed others to help me fight.

Paul was a good fighter. He let Timothy know that he had fought the good fight. He had not gotten anyone else to fight for him, and he had not gathered a crowd to fight with him. He had fought his own battles. He had finished the race, and he had kept the faith. He knew that a crown of righteousness was reserved for him.

What about us? Is there a crown reserved for us? Although we may not be good fist fighters, we ought to be good faith fighters. We must have faith to sustain us when Satan is at work in our lives. We must have faith to support others during their difficult days. We must have faith to speak the word of truth when no one believes it or even wants to hear it. We must have faith to endure to the end.

Paul finished his course. He knew his departure was near but was not worried about his future. He was ready to receive his crown. Will our fighting be good enough to join him?

Lord, equip me with faith to fight for you until I finish my course. Amen.

GRACE AND MERCY

TITUS 3:1-7

*He saved us, not because of any works of
righteousness that we had done, but according
to his mercy, through the water of rebirth and
renewal by the Holy Spirit. (Titus 3:5)*

In this letter to Titus, Paul gives sound advice
to all ministers of the gospel. If there are any questions about obeying the governmental laws, he
writes, "remind them to be subject to rulers and
authorities, to be obedient, to be ready for every
good work" (3:1). There should never be a question
concerning our responsibilities as Christians to be
obedient to the laws that govern us. We even need
to make every attempt to participate in the making
of laws and in serving our juries. We can do good

work as politicians and as citizens who perform our civic duties.

Paul further reminds Titus to tell the people "to speak evil of no one, to avoid quarreling, to be gentle, and to show every courtesy to everyone" (3:2). What a difference it would make in the world if we just heeded this advice. It sounds a lot like the Golden Rule, but we don't pay much attention to it either. Perhaps our ministers need to keep reminding us just as Paul encouraged Titus to remind the people.

Then Paul encourages us all to remember the past God has brought us from. We were not always saved. We once participated in foolish and disobedient acts and were slaves to our passions and pleasures. We are not so far removed from that time that we can sit in judgment of others, for it was God's grace and mercy that has saved us. We have done nothing to earn God's grace. God's goodness and love have made our salvation possible.

Paul knew that Titus needed to remind the people in Crete of these things; and we, the people in other parts of the world, need to be reminded also. It is God's grace and mercy that has saved us. Praise be to God!

Lord, I thank you for your grace and mercy. Keep me mindful of my obligation to be ready for every good work. Amen.

AN IMPASSIONED PLEA

PHILEMON

I am appealing to you for my child, Onesimus,
whose father I have become during my
imprisonment. (Philemon 10)

𝕸ost of us can relate to making an impassioned plea for our children. If there was somewhere our children wanted to be included, but we feared that they would be rejected, we would make an emotional appeal. This might be especially true if we knew that we would be accepted in that place. We might even do what Paul did and say, "So if you consider me your partner, welcome him as you would welcome me" (v. 17).

Whenever we make a request like this, we are putting our reputations and ourselves on the line. We are saying that we stand behind the person for whom we are pleading and that we will be responsible for that person's having been accepted. Paul made it perfectly clear by his statement, "If he has wronged you in any way, or owes you anything, charge that to my account" (v. 18). Now, we might be willing to do this for a child, but would we do it for anyone else?

I have often been asked to write letters of recommendation for students who were applying for a job or a scholarship. I have told them that my recommendation will not mean anything in the future if they do not perform according to the highest standards. I want to recommend only people whom I feel confident about and know very well.

Paul felt confident about Onesimus. Paul had lived with him and had found him to be of valuable service. So he could request or even demand that the former slave be accepted as a brother. But Paul would not do that. He wanted Philemon willingly and graciously to accept Onesimus.

When we are moved to make impassioned pleas, I am sure that we want the plea to be accepted and willingly acted upon. We want to retain our good standing with the person to whom we made the plea. We want to be able to request with Paul that a guest room be prepared for us.

Lord, make me willing to plea with passion for those children of yours who need my assistance in being accepted just as they are. Amen.

ASSURANCE THROUGH FAITH

HEBREWS 11

Now faith is the assurance of things hoped for, the conviction of things not seen. (Hebrews 11:1)

What blessed assurance to know that things hoped for and unseen really exist! Such knowledge is blessed assurance indeed, and it is the essence of our faith. Our faith gives hope when we have no reason to hope. Our faith gives proof when there is no proof. Our faith is what believers base their lives on.

It was faith that Lori needed when, six weeks from the expected due date of her first child, she started to feel labor pains. She knew that it was too soon, but she could not ignore the pains. So she checked into the hospital, was given medication in an effort to stop the contractions, and was put on complete bed rest. But the baby would not be denied. She was born anyway.

The doctors had prophesied gloom and doom. They told Lori that the baby would have little chance for survival, but she believed that God would save her baby. Lori asked her family to pray and to have faith that her baby daughter would survive. She thought of her ninety-three-year-old grandmother who had lived her long life on faith. There had been times in her grandmother's life when she did not have food to feed her family. During those times God provided the money to buy the next meal. It was her great faith that assured her that God would provide again. Lori needed faith like that of her grandmother.

The baby weighed five pounds and had no difficulty breathing. It was just as the family of faith had predicted. The evidence seen was that the tiny baby would have underdeveloped lungs, but faith, the evidence of things not seen, produced a small baby with developed lungs. The healthy baby was the substance of things hoped for.

Lord, I have read numerous examples of men and women of faith, from Abel to Abraham to Moses to so many more. I know their testimonies; help me develop a faith and a testimony like theirs. Amen.

❧

PRISONERS OR SINNERS?

HEBREWS 13:1-6

Remember those who are in prison, as though you were in prison with them; those who are being tortured, as though you yourselves were being tortured. (Hebrews 13:3)

I often teach Bible study classes at the Georgia Metro State Prison for Women. Many of the women do not consider themselves to be prisoners; but they recognize that they are sinners. They have sinned, broken the law of the state and the law of God, and they have been caught. Even though they are being punished for their crimes and their sins, they insist on being treated as children of God.

Whenever I go to the prison, I am reminded that we all have sinned and fallen short of the glory of God. After listening to some of the reasons for their crimes, I know that many of us could have been incarcerated with these women. So I can relate as though I were in prison with them.

Once, I led a class on the Apocrypha, the books between the Old and New Testaments. The Prayer of Manasseh was special for one woman who had murdered her eight-year-old son's rapist. Manasseh was king of Jerusalem for fifty-five years. He was an evil king, but he repented. Although the story of his reign and repentance are recorded in 2 Chronicles 33, his prayer is recorded in the Apocrypha. In that prayer, Manasseh humbly repents and says, "I bend the knee of my heart." That phrase conjures up a picture of total humility, and that is the way this woman, also a repentant sinner, approached God.

I asked the other women if they had ever bowed the knee of their hearts before God and confessed that I had. When I made that confession, I won the heart of that particular prisoner. She told me that so many people who came to the prison did not identify with them and pretended that they could never be incarcerated. I let her know that not only could I pray Manasseh's prayer, but also I could pray her prayer.

Lord, I bend the knee of my heart before you. Amen.

❧

THE DUAL TONGUE

JAMES 3:1-12

With it we bless the Lord and Father, and with it we curse those who are made in the likeness of God. (James 3:9)

𝒯he tongue is a dual weapon. It can kill with kindness and with meanness. It can bless, and it can curse. Unrestrained, it can be dangerous; controlled, it can be a powerful agent.

James wrote some compelling words about the tongue. He wrote that the tongue controls the body, for even though it is a small member, it boasts of great exploits. It can tame beast, bird, reptile, and sea creature, "but no one can tame the tongue—a restless evil, full of deadly poison" (3:8).

These words became very real to me as I consoled

a young bride who had a vicious encounter with her mother-in-law. The mother-in-law told the bride that she was not good enough for her son. She was not pretty or smart or rich, and there was no way to understand what spell had been cast over her son to convince him to marry her. The mother-in-law even admitted that she had picked out someone else worthy of her son. Needless to say, that mother and daughter-in-law relationship was damaged beyond repair.

It did no good for me to try to convince the bride that the mother-in-law did not mean what she had said. The words had been spoken; the tongue had spewed its deadly poison. Their future relationship would have been so different if that mother-in-law had kept her feelings to herself or if she had spoken welcoming words to the bride. She might have preferred that her son had chosen someone else, but it was not her decision. She should have tried to be cordial.

Words once spoken cannot be retrieved. We need to think before we speak and use our tongues to bless and not curse.

Lord, I know that I am not perfect and that I will make mistakes as I speak with my brothers and sisters. But help me be kind. Amen.

☙

FAILING TO ASK

JAMES 4:1-10

You want something and do not have it; so you commit murder. And you covet something and cannot obtain it; so you engage in disputes and conflicts. You do not have, because you do not ask. (James 4:2)

Whenever I ask for something and am surprised to get it, I am reminded of the words, "You do not have, because you do not ask." I wonder how many blessings we miss because we do not ask. Asking involves risk taking. We must be aware that denial is always an option. However, if we do not ask, we will never know what the answer would have been.

Yet, we must be aware of the spirit in which we ask. The passage from James lists the sins that have resulted from worldly desires. He warned that one who sought to be satisfied by the world would be an enemy of God. Many of the material things that were desired were not received because they were not asked for in the right way. Things were requested for worldly pleasure, but God desired requests made in humility with the spirit that he had made to dwell in his people. How different our requests would be if they were made in humility with a godlike spirit.

Before you ask God for anything, think about how you will respond if your request is granted. There are ministers who ask for larger churches and doctors who ask for larger practices and many who simply ask for greater wealth. Why are they asking for these things? What will the minister do with the larger church? Will he or she be a better pastor? Is that minister faithfully serving the members he or she already has? What if that doctor gets a larger practice? Will he or she become a better doctor? Will the time available to his or her patients be shortened? If any of us had more money, what would we do with it? What spirit dwells in us as we ask?

God is able to do abundantly more than we dare to think or ask, but he expects something from us. Are we willing to give it?

Lord, I promise to make my requests known to you in a spirit of humility and love. Amen.

❧

HAVE YOU MET THE LION?

1 PETER 5:1-11

Discipline yourselves, keep alert. Like a roaring lion your adversary the devil prowls around, looking for someone to devour. (1 Peter 5:8)

If you are serious about practicing your religion, you have met the lion. The lion prowls around, hoping to devour you in your weakest moment. Of course, this lion is the devil, and he does not want you to be a faithful servant of the Lord. He can disguise himself in many ways. He may be a church member, a friend, a beautiful woman, or a handsome man. Whatever form he takes, he is the devil, and he is waiting to meet you.

When I taught college-level religion courses, students often told me that they were progressing nicely in every way before joining the church. They said that they had sufficient finances, were making good grades, had good friends, and were generally pleased with life. After making a decision to affiliate with a church, everything started to change. They had to struggle to pay their bills; their grades started to drop; their friends no longer wanted to associate with them; and they often were depressed. They wanted to know what had happened. I let them know that they had met the lion.

The lion, the devil, waited to meet them and had no need to devour them as long as they were serving him. The devil could relax as long as they were not worshiping God. They were his servants if they never rendered praise and thanksgiving to God. The devil did not have to use their friends to convince them to hang out in the recreation center and avoid the library. The devil was happy, and so were they.

Peter warned of the devil's lurking around and looking for those who were weak in the faith. The devil, then and now, wants to reclaim any servants that have been lost to God. We have to resist the devil and remain steadfast in our faith. We will suffer, but we will be delivered. We can be assured that others have suffered and have emerged stronger in the faith. Expect to meet the lion head-on, but be prepared to fight him with faith.

Lord, I know the lion is waiting. Equip me to fight him with faith. Amen.

Everything We Need

2 Peter 1:3-11

His divine power has given us everything needed
for life and godliness, through the knowledge of
him who called us by his own glory and goodness.
(2 Peter 1:3)

Wouldn't it be wonderful to have everything we need? Most of the time we really do have everything we need, but we do not have everything we want. Our wants usually include the material things we could easily do without, and sometimes we get the things we want and still are not satisfied. We always want more.

But Peter writes that knowing God and responding to his glory and goodness equips us with everything we need for life and godliness. If we have what we need to live and to be godly, what more is there?

Let's think about it. If God grants us life, we are well on our way to having what we need. If we are not alive, there is nothing we can do to respond to God's glory and goodness. To serve God in this life, we need to be alive, and we who are reading this meditation have life.

If we are to be godly, we must know God. God loved us so much that he sent his Son to teach us how to be godly. We must know God and study to show ourselves approved unto him. So many so-called Christians do not know what Jesus taught and do not study their Bibles. I wonder how many worshipers attend church without their Bibles. How can they study and digest the Word when they have left the Word at home?

Knowing God through our Lord and Savior Jesus Christ, studying the Bible, and constantly seeking a right relationship with both God and our fellow human beings equip us to live godly, sober lives, and that is everything we need.

Lord, I know you have provided all that I need. Thank you. Amen.

DO YOU NEED
TO HEAR THE WORDS?

1 JOHN 3:11-24; 4:7-21

Little children, let us love, not in word or speech,
but in truth and action. (1 John 3:18)

y husband often says that he does not need to keep telling me that he loves me but that he shows it by what he does for me. He loves to shop, and he enjoys buying things for me. He makes sure that I am aware of and included in all of his activities and schedules time for family vacations and family nights. Each unexpected gift or act of kindness is a declaration of his love.

He also says that I show my love for him by preparing meals carefully. He will boast that no matter how late he comes home, even if I have already gone to bed, I will get up and fix his dinner. He loves to tell the other preachers on his staff that I prepare his breakfast before he leaves for the 8 A.M. worship service every Sunday. My taking care of his need for food and comfort are my acts of love.

John informed his readers that we love in truth and action. Words are empty when they are not supported by deeds. By loving one another, we show that we know God, for God is love. We lie when we claim our love for God, whom we have never seen, and hate our brothers and sisters, whom we see daily.

I wonder how many of us have sought to live by these words. What about that unfair boss we cannot stand? What about that interracial couple we do not feel belongs in our neighborhood? What about that homosexual couple that dares to attend our church? Aren't these the people that we see every day and are supposed to love? Isn't our love to be in deeds and in truth and not just in words? Does God really live in us?

Remember John's words, "No one has ever seen God; if we love one another, God lives in us, and his love is perfected in us" (4:12).

Lord, I want to show my love for you by loving my brothers and sisters even when I really don't like what they do. Help me love them into repentance. Amen.

❧

ON GUARD

2 JOHN

Be on your guard, so that you do not lose what we have worked for, but may receive a full reward.
(2 John 8)

$\mathcal{D}$id you realize that this letter is written to the elect lady and her children? John gives this noble lady great respect and confesses that he and all who know the truth love her. What a wonderful salutation!

John continues the letter by announcing his joy in finding some of this dear lady's children walking in truth just as they have been commanded; however, he wants to make sure that they remember to love one another as well. It seems that John is very much aware that even though we keep the commandments we sometimes fail really to love one another. Haven't you met people who never really do anything wrong, but they are cold and unfeeling. They do not know how to express love.

The love that we as Christians ought to feel for one another must be genuine for there will be many deceivers who do not believe that Jesus came in the flesh to save us from our sins. We must be on guard against them and the lack of truth they represent. If we listen to them and choose to follow their ways, we will lose all that we have worked for. Keeping the commandments will not save us if we do not believe that Jesus is the Christ.

John warns the elect lady and her children to stay away from those who do not believe. He even tells them not to welcome unbelievers into their house. They must be on guard. This warning is also for us. I know that we warn our children about people who may want to associate with them and lead them into lives of crime, but are we guarding against those who want to lead them away from Christ? Our love and knowledge of God act as a shield of protection to help us guard against those who would lead us astray. We are reminded to watch as well as to pray.

Lord, thank you for those who live in truth and love. Put those people in my path, and let me walk with them. Amen.

TALKING FACE-TO-FACE

3 JOHN

*I hope to see you soon, and we will talk together
face to face. (3 John 14)*

How technology has changed since John wrote this letter to Gaius, his son in the ministry. But even then, John realized that the written letter could not substitute for being able to talk face-to-face. In this modern day, we have telephones, video conferencing, E-mail, and posted mail; but there is still nothing like talking to a person face-to-face. We can not only see that person, but also touch him or her.

What does talking face-to-face add to the conversation? Well, we can watch the facial expressions, the body language, the vocal inflections, but most important of all we can reach out and touch each other. A harsh word can be softened by a loving touch. A smile can help convey the sincerity in a statement, and the body can move in such a way that communication is obvious without words.

John probably wanted to touch Gaius when he commended him for his hospitality and faithfulness to the truth, and he probably would have frowned and shaken his finger as he spoke about Diotrephes, who was spreading false charges and failing to walk in truth. Then he probably would have smiled again when he spoke of Demetrius, about whom there was a good report.

Wouldn't it be wonderful to have face-to-face conversations with Christians who walk in truth? We could look into their faces and know that all they told us was true. We could trust their words and follow their examples. Do you think we could qualify as just such a Christian?

Lord, I want to have a face-to-face conversation with someone who is walking in truth. Help me be a person with whom others can have such a conversation. Amen.

CENTERED BY GOD'S LOVE

JUDE 17-23

Keep yourselves in the love of God; look forward to the mercy of our Lord Jesus Christ that leads to eternal life. (Jude 21)

What does it mean to be centered by God's love? As I read Jude's letter, I believe it means to stay in the middle of God's love surrounded by faith, mercy, hope, and prayer. Imagine yourself as the center of a circle. On the circumference of the circle you see the faith you have. Next to faith there is mercy, and you know that mercy takes up a large area because God is so merciful to us. Next to mercy is hope, and hope is a solid part of the circle of love. Prayer is next to hope because we pray with hope that our prayers will be answered.

Now let us remain in the center of God's love while the circle revolves around us. Each day we need faith to work actively. We can reach out and touch it as it revolves around us. We also notice mercy as it passes by. We keep grasping for mercy because we know that we do not deserve it, but it is a part of God's love. We try to stop hope as it revolves by because we need hope to continue on our journey. Then prayer revolves past, and we remember that we need to be constant in prayer. As we remain in the center of God's love, we can actively grab faith, mercy, hope, and prayer. We are not distracted by false teachers and idle dreamers.

Those who remain in the center of God's love and are strengthened by the elements on the circumference must be aware of others who are not solidly centered. We are charged to snatch them from the fire (vv. 22-23). We want everyone to be secure in God's love. We must try to bring others to the center with us so that we all can look forward to the mercy of our Lord Jesus Christ that leads to eternal life. It would be tragic if we were the only ones who had an opportunity to enjoy eternal life. Stay in the center of God's love; and once you are secure and solidly grounded, reach out for your brother and sisters.

Lord, I want to be centered by your love. Amen.

❧

HEAVEN

REVELATION 21

*He will wipe every tear from their eyes. Death
will be no more; mourning and crying and pain
will be no more, for the first things have passed
away. (Revelation 21:4)*

I remember a little girl who went to Disney
World with her parents. She was so happy to be
there and to see the beautiful world created in
Orlando that she asked her mother if heaven would
be like that. Her mother smiled as she thought that
for her daughter, heaven would seem like Disney
World.

Little did that mother know that in less than a
month, her daughter would be in heaven. One
Sunday during the church service, a tornado killed
her daughter and others. That mother remembered

the child's words and was content knowing that her child was in the Disney World that is heaven. She could rejoice knowing that Jesus is there to wipe every tear away. No one in heaven ever dies, and there is no crying or pain. Her daughter is happy—for the first things—the things of this earth, have passed away.

John carefully describes the holy city that he sees. It is a beautiful city adorned like a bride for her husband. Everything is made new, and those who dwell there are God's children. Those who live in this beautiful city are conquerors, and they enjoy the grandeur that surrounds them. There are walls of jasper with foundations of every jewel. There are streets of gold, and the light is provided by the glory of God. Jesus, the Lamb, is its lamp. Oh, what a beautiful city!

We have an opportunity to join the Father and the Son in that beautiful city. We prepare ourselves to live there eternally by obeying the commandments and by making the gospel that Jesus taught a part of our daily lives. One glad morning this earthly life will be over, and we will fly away. Don't you want to meet that heavenly host of angels who will greet you with loud Hallelujahs? I do.

Holy Father, help me live so that one day I will see that beautiful city that will be my eternal home. Amen.